D1565904

Andrew Johnson,
17th President of the United States,
painted in 1866 by David Acheson Woodward

President Andrew Johnson of Greeneville, Tennessee

by

Robert Orr

TENNESSEE VALLEY
Publishing®

2005

Copyright © 2005

Published by

Tennessee Valley Publishing,
P.O. Box 52527,
Knoxville, Tennessee 37950-2527
www.TVP1.com

Cover art: "Civil War Greeneville," from Nathanael Greene Museum, painted by Joe Kilday, Dell Hughes and Robert Orr. Also, President Andrew Johnson portrait by Mathew Brady.

Printed and bound in the United States of America.

Library of Congress Cataloging-in-Publication Data

Orr, Robert, 1942
    President Andrew Johnson of Greeneville, Tennessee / Robert Orr
          p. cm.
    Includes bibliographical references.
    ISBN: 1-932604-15-4
    1. Johnson, Andrew, 1808-1875. 2. Presidents–United States–Biography. 3. United States–Politics and government–1845-1861. 4. United States–Politics and government–1861-1865. 5. United States–Politics and government–1865-1877. 6. Greeneville (Tenn.)–Biography. I. Title
      E667.O77 2005
      973.8'1'092–dc22

                    2005005554

Contents

List of Illustrations

List of Illustrations (continued)

Margaret Patterson Bartlett

Foreword

During the time the United States has been in existence, there have only been 43 Presidents of the United States. The Town of Greeneville, Tennessee should be very proud of the fact that one of them is a native son of our Town.

Our Town has also been blessed by the remarkable life of an amazing lady, Margaret Johnson Patterson Bartlett, who was the great-granddaughter of President Andrew Johnson. Mrs. Bartlett devoted her life to the greater good of her fellow man and to a better understanding of President Andrew Johnson. Under her Will, most of her estate went to the Bartlett-Patterson Corporation, a non-profit corporation that she directed be established for the purpose of improving the lives of the people of Greeneville and Greene County, and promoting understanding of President Andrew Johnson.

By commissioning and publishing this biography of President Andrew Johnson, the corporation is furthering its work in the fulfillment of Mrs. Bartlett's wishes.

Mrs. Bartlett sought no recognition for herself. However, it is appropriate that Mrs. Bartlett be recognized for her wisdom, foresight and generosity.

We are very proud of the scholarship and story telling ability of our author, Dr. Robert Orr. Thank you, Bob, for a great read.

Gene Gaby, President
C. Ray Adams, Secretary-Treasurer
BARTLETT-PATTERSON CORPORATION

Preface

I began the study of Andrew Johnson as part of a lifelong interest in East Tennessee and the Civil War. In my youth the war was a living memory: I met one of the last surviving veterans. The stories I heard from older generations were often stories they had heard from the participants. The Civil War in East Tennessee was a war of secret societies and close escapes: the area "changed hands" many times. This struggle of brigades of cavalry, irregulars, and secret societies is a little known aspect of Andrew Johnson's life that will be explored here. Although he was absent from East Tennessee from 1861 to 1869, he was in contact with many Unionists who lived in Confederate East Tennessee. For Johnson during the war, these contacts were an opportunity. In the post-war period, Johnson felt an obligation not to abandon his Southern Unionist allies. And he stood by them, to the great annoyance of the Radical Republicans, his major political opponents. Recent studies largely ignore the Greene County and East Tennessee background of Johnson's career. The Civil War in East Tennessee and the desire of East Tennesseans to free the slaves are given slight attention. The East Tennessee emancipationist movement lasted from the pioneer days to the acts of emancipation in the 1860s: Johnson was influenced by this movement, and indeed he fulfilled it when he proclaimed freedom for the Tennessee slaves in October 1864.

Many family members have told me stories of the Civil War and Reconstruction era. I have also discussed the topic with Margaret Patterson Bartlett, great granddaughter of Andrew Johnson, and Ralph Phinney, Margaret's first cousin. Two historians of Greeneville and Greene County, Richard Doughty and Harry Roberts, have discussed with me the life of Andrew Johnson and how local traditions molded his life and outlook.

I wish to thank Mark Corey and Jim Small of the National Park Service, Andrew Johnson Site for the use of the Park Service's small but excellent library and archives, and for their knowledge and objectivity in reading drafts of this work. Many of the photographs included in this work are from the Park Service Collection.

I wish to thank the staff of the Tusculum College Library for their assistance, and the college's President Andrew Johnson Museum and Library (Old College) for the use of the David Acheson Woodward painting of Andrew Johnson. I am indebted to the staff of the Greeneville-Greene County Public Library and the T. Elmer Cox Historical and Genealogical Library for their assistance, and the staff of the Special Collections Library of the University of Tennessee, Knoxville, and the Calvin M. McClung Historical Collection, Knox County Public Library for their assistance. I would like to thank the staff of the Tennessee State Library and Archives for their assistance. I also wish to thank Steven K. Harbison for his work in copying and organizing the photographs which are included in this volume.

Two people in the text are relatives of mine. Major James H. Robinson, Confederate Provost Marshal of Greene County, is my great, great grandfather and was a pallbearer in Johnson's funeral. Oliver Temple, the noted author, attorney and wartime Unionist, is my great, great, great uncle.

I would like to thank the Bartlett-Patterson Corporation for proposing this biographical study of President Johnson with an emphasis on Greeneville and Greene County's many influences on his life, and especially the editing and suggestions of Ray Adams and Gene Gaby. Although the original project was a book for school children, I hope there is enough new material to interest the general public. Where documents are quoted, the original spelling and punctuation has been retained.

This book is dedicated to all who have helped preserve the oral traditions of East Tennessee in the Civil War and Reconstruction.

Robert Orr

Robert Orr
March, 2005

**Andrew Johnson Statue,
by Jim Gray**

Chapter One
Young Andrew Johnson

Andrew Johnson was seventeen years old when he left North Carolina with his mother and stepfather, bound for Tennessee. The year was 1826. They came from Raleigh, North Carolina, and crossed into Tennessee by way of Paint Rock, North Carolina. The Paint Creek Road they followed emerges from the mountains into the broad, fertile valley of East Tennessee.

Johnson and his family approached Greeneville by the Warm Springs Road (now called the Old Asheville Highway) which was the main road from North Carolina in the area. His mother Mary rode in a two-wheel cart, while Andrew and his stepfather Turner Daughtry led the blind pony that pulled the cart. Greene County was sparsely populated in 1826, with dirt roads and large areas of virgin timber. The travelers passed log, frame and brick homes along the road through Greene County. The farms had log and weatherboard barns and outbuildings. The gardens, yards and fields were enclosed by angular, split rail fences. Cattle were branded and turned loose to roam the range: fences were built to keep cattle out, not in.

As Johnson and his family neared town, they passed Greeneville College, a cluster of large buildings to the right of the road. In later years, Johnson often walked the three miles from town to the college to attend the debating society. Johnson and his family arrived at the edge of town and camped in a field at the spring below the present-day Andrew Johnson Homestead on Main Street. The road they had traveled crossed "Brown's Hill" just outside of town, and Johnson got fodder from the Browns that evening. From their camp, Andrew Johnson could see the village of Greeneville uphill to the east.

The next day was Sunday, and Johnson walked into the peaceful village "with quick determined steps, indicative of the powerful will within." His arrival in Greeneville was described by Oliver P. Temple, a resident of Greene County at the time. "The atmosphere was laden with the perfume of honeysuckles and wild roses. From the neat gardens cultivated flowers shed their fragrance on the soft air. Greeneville, at all times lovely, was never more so than on that bright May morning, as it lay in solemn stillness flooded with light, nestling serenely among its green hills." Although Temple mentions a "bright May morning," most modern historians assert that Johnson arrived in September—controversy surrounds Andrew Johnson, beginning with the day he first set foot in Greeneville.

Temple's word portrait of the town included the gentle sound of "water falling from the race-head of a little mill that stood at the foot of a great hill south of the town." This description of the Greeneville's picturesque little gristmill has led some to state that Greeneville was a "milltown." Others have called it a "mountain town." Both descriptions are incorrect. Greeneville in the 1820s was a prosperous, stately little village of a few hundred residents in the great valley of East Tennessee, a valley formed by the Appalachian and Cumberland Mountains.

The town of 1826 had several large brick and frame buildings. The Greene County Courthouse and the larger homes and churches had elaborate carpentry and masonry: finished lumber had been produced locally since the first decade of the nineteenth century, and brick before that. Some of the larger frame homes were painted white; most were unpainted, and there were many log cabins in the town. Most buildings were located so that their front doors opened directly onto the street. Hitching posts and board sidewalks were found here and there. There was regular stagecoach and mail service with the rest of the country.

The town covered about six blocks from just beyond the "Big Spring," the town water supply, to the houses uphill from where Johnson and his family had camped. The little village centered around the Dickson Williams Mansion, which fronted Main Street behind a formal garden and pleasure grounds, covering the entire block.

Johnson was young, healthy, with a quick mind, and he was skilled at his trade. His family was poor. He had been apprenticed as a boy to a tailor in Raleigh, his hometown. He ran away from the apprenticeship and wandered through South Carolina and Alabama. Andrew was a hard worker, and he liked to recall that when he picked cotton on his journey through the Deep South, he picked more cotton than the experienced workers.

In Greeneville, Johnson soon met Eliza McCardle, who helped him find a cabin for his family. Eliza has been described as a "typical Scotch lassie, her nut-brown hair played around an ample forehead, her eyes were soft hazel."

Andrew and Eliza noticed each other when he first walked into Greeneville in 1826. They would be married within a year. Johnson found work with the town tailor, Robert Maloney. Johnson wanted his own shop and moved to nearby Rutledge, where he lived and worked for a few months. He returned to Greeneville to stay in 1827. He had heard that Mr. Maloney had retired. Johnson knew that he could now be Greeneville's only tailor.

Eliza McCardle Johnson

On May 17, 1827, Andrew Johnson and Eliza McCardle were married in a ceremony in Warrensburg, a village in the western part of the county. Eliza's father had been a cobbler in Warrensburg when he died some years before. At their marriage, Andrew was 18 and Eliza was 16. The retiring tailor, Robert Maloney, signed the marriage bond.

Youngest photograph of Andrew Johnson

Johnson's first tailor shop in Greeneville was in a log building on Main Street. He lived with his family in a room in the back. Their first two children, Martha and Charles, were born in the log home on Main Street. Andrew Johnson worked long hours and made good, sturdy clothes. While living in his Main Street home, he began to study Eliza's textbooks from the Greeneville Female Academy. He had learned the basics of reading before leaving North Carolina, but Eliza taught him how to write.

An early Andrew Johnson signature,
written on the title page of a book Eliza gave him

Johnson made friends with the students of Greeneville College, who came to him for repairs to their clothes. They found that he was as interested in their studies as they were. He would pay them pennies to read their textbooks to him while he sewed. He was soon visiting the college and attending functions.

Greeneville College in those days consisted of three large buildings on a hill where today there is only a clump of trees and a large sandstone marker by the roadside. The buildings of Andrew Johnson's day included a two-story main building, covered with weatherboard outside and paneling and ceiling inside. There were classrooms, a library, chimneys at either end, and a small cupola on the roof. A two-story brick rooming house nearby provided rooms for the resident students. The president's house was a weatherboard house with an elaborate stone foundation and basement, and a stone chimney. The college would soon give Andrew Johnson a grounding in moral philosophy that would never leave him.

Greeneville College had been founded by one of the leaders of the East Tennessee emancipationist movement, Dr. Hezekiah Balch. Dr. Balch had established an unusually liberal admissions policy during the early years of the school, which had been founded in 1794. Dr. Balch admitted Indians, women and at least one black student, a young man named John Gloucester, who went on to become a Presbyterian minister.

The second President of Greeneville College was Dr. Charles Coffin, who was also an emancipationist. The college continued to

Johnson's home during the 1830s and 1840s,
at the corner of Depot and College Streets, in those days, the Second Cross Street and Water Street

have faculty and guest scholars who advocated freedom for the slaves, one of these stating in a speech at the college in 1824: "When slavery rears her sickly head among the habitations of men, how debasing the effects she spreads around!"

Johnson became a regular participant at the college debating society even though he never officially enrolled in the school. The liberal policy on attendance had remained under the third college president, Dr. Henry Hoss, who was president when Johnson attended the college debating society. Johnson was hesitant at first about public speaking, but he possessed a "natural talent for oratory." Once over his shyness, he became an effective speaker and an aggressive debater.

A word portrait of Dr. Hoss comes from the year 1833, when Sam Milligan, a young Greene County lad, walked up to the college carrying everything that he owned and having very little money. He was fearful he was not qualified to attend the school. Milligan was welcomed by Dr. Hoss, and recalled that his "address was so gentle and kind, that I felt at ease in his presence, and at once became strongly attached to him." Milligan was allowed to enter the school by promising to pay his tuition after he graduated and made some money. Sam Milligan and Andrew Johnson soon met and became lifelong friends. They were political allies and both became Unionists when the Civil War tore the country apart in the 1860s.

Johnson was successful at his trade, and by 1831 he had saved enough money to buy a brick home on Water Street. Greeneville's street names have changed since Johnson bought his brick home at the corner of Water Street and the Second Cross Street. Main Street was where it is today. Church Street was called the Third Cross Street; Depot Street was the Second Cross Street, and Summer Street was the First Cross Street. College Street was called Water Street, because Richland Creek often flooded the lower section of the street. During a hard rain, the lower end of Water Street would be under water.

Tailor Shop photograph, thought to be 1865

That same year, 1831, Johnson bought a small frame shop on Main Street. The owner sold the building, but not the lot where it sat, so Johnson had to move the building. He and a few friends lifted the shop onto logs they had laid out in the street. Then they began slowly to roll the building, bringing the rear log around to the front of the building as they progressed. Using ropes to guide the building, they successfully rolled it to a lot Johnson owned at the corner of Water Street and the Second Cross Street, down the hill behind the courthouse. About the same time, Johnson moved into the brick home across the street from the Tailor Shop.

The little frame building at the corner of Water Street and the Second Cross Street became Johnson's Tailor Shop, and there he hung his shingle "A. Johnson, Tailor." The Tailor Shop sits today where Johnson located it, except that now the little frame shop sits inside a brick building at the corner of College Street and Depot Street.

People liked and trusted Johnson, and his success in moving the shop building led to other jobs moving buildings. He was open and friendly, and soon became popular as "Andy" Johnson, the stylish new tailor who loved to talk politics. He hired others to sew while he measured and cut cloth. He advised his workers: "Save something. Get you a home." Two more children were born while the Johnsons lived in the new brick home on Water Street: Mary and Robert.

In 1829, Andrew Johnson stood for election as alderman of the town and was elected. He held various local offices and was elected Mayor in 1834. All this time, Johnson prospered. He was a good businessman, keeping careful records of profits and expenses. He approached government service the same way. The people liked his frugal approach, and he was reelected many times to local and state offices.

In 1834, while Johnson was serving as Mayor of Greeneville, a Tennessee Constitutional Convention was held in Nashville to revise the state constitution, which had been written in 1796. Thirty Tennessee counties sent petitions to the convention asking that slavery be outlawed in the state of Tennessee. Most of the petitions came from East Tennessee, where there were few commercial slave plantations.

Greene County sent two emancipationist petitions to Nashville, and they contained more names than any other county's petitions. Although Johnson did not sign these petitions, he was Mayor at the time and would have been aware of the strong sentiment in Greene County in favor of emancipation. He had attended the debates at Greeneville College, where emancipation was a long held commitment. The intellectual climate of Greeneville and Greene County strongly influenced Johnson toward a belief in freedom for the slaves, and Johnson in later years would say that he had "always" opposed slavery.

Johnson's popularity and success in local politics led him to consider running for higher office. On a Saturday night in one of Greeneville's gathering places during 1835, Johnson was listening to a discussion of an upcoming race for State Representative. On an impulse, Johnson stood and said, "Boys, count me in the fight too!"

The race was for "floater," as they called it: a State Representative who represented both Greene County and neighboring Washington County—thus he floated between two counties. The officeholder was Matthew Stephenson from Washington County, whose county seat was Jonesborough. Stephenson was a well-respected man who had introduced a motion to make Tennessee a free state (that is, free of slavery) to the 1834 constitutional convention.

Johnson and Stephenson apparently did not debate slavery: both were against it. But Johnson had a winning issue in his passion for economy in government. In these early debates, he was remembered as saying: "There are no good laws but such as repeal other laws." He was elected, and now, besides being a successful tailor, "Andy" Johnson was a "floater" in the State Legislature.

Johnson loved the freedom from government interference of the American lifestyle, and he believed the American people should be left free. The national government was small, inexpensive and had very little contact with people's everyday lives. Slavery existed, as it had around the world since Biblical times, but the reformers thought slavery would eventually be ended by state action, as it had been in most Northern states.

During the years of Johnson's early political contests, most East Tennesseans were in favor of the emancipation of slaves. In Nashville during his first term in the State Legislature, he began a lifetime advocacy of the cause of emancipation. A law was proposed to ban abolitionist literature from the mail. Johnson voted against the law. The bill passed, and abolitionist literature was banned from the mail in Tennessee. Despite this defeat, he continued to advocate emancipation of the slaves by any legal means.

Young Andrew Johnson

In 1839, as a State Representative, he took part in an act of emancipation, the first of many during his life. Tennessee law at the time was that slaves who were freed by their owner must leave the state. Johnson forwarded a petition to the state legislature from two of his constituents asking that they be allowed to free two of their slaves, who would then marry and remain in Tennessee.

Johnson became a Democrat after briefly associating with the Whig Party. The Whigs were the political party of the aristocracy and of larger central government: two ideas that did not appeal to Johnson. His basic political goals were to bring the working class into the political system, and to improve—to "ameliorate" as Johnson liked to say—their living conditions. These were his primary political goals, and he accepted emancipation of slaves as a part of these goals.

As a Democrat, Johnson was always something of a maverick, and he gave little support to the Democratic Party's principle that the nation's money should be only gold and silver coins. This principle was written into the U.S. Constitution in the provision that Congress has the power to "coin money," but not to print it. Today, paper money (the "dollar bill") is taken for granted, but it was not in Johnson's time. There was no national paper money until the Civil War in the 1860s, and even then many people opposed the policy of issuing paper money. The question of what should be the nation's money—coins or paper money—left Johnson in an ambiguous position. He wanted in all things to go by the Constitution, but he realized that a strictly metal currency would leave the lower classes without enough money. Johnson's lifelong purpose was to help the lower classes improve themselves. Faced with an unsolvable dilemma, he moved on to other issues, and let others debate the currency question.

Johnson served several terms in the State Legislature, pursuing economy in government and public funding of grade schools for Tennessee children. He lost only once, in 1837, and that was because he opposed state aid to a railroad through East Tennessee. In 1839 he beat the man who had defeated him two years before, and Johnson did not lose another political race until after the Civil War.

In 1841, Johnson became a State Senator, and his success in elections gave him a growing prominence in the Democratic Party. He held large rallies at the Greene County Courthouse, and the people came from great distances to hear him speak. Most of his supporters were farmers, who came from near and far along the roads and by-ways of Greene County in increasingly large groups until they arrived in Greeneville where an immense crowd filled the downtown streets. Johnson's supporters would pile large boxes against the wall of the courthouse, where he would stand and speak for three or four hours. His speeches had familiar themes. He sketched the political history of the country: how the Federalist Party of George Washington's day had been for a strong central government, and the party of Jefferson, which became the Democratic Party, had been for local control of most issues. Now the Whig Party had arisen and was advocating a strong central government, but the Democrats were still for local control. Johnson believed that people should be left free to live their own lives, and the independent farmers of East Tennessee agreed and loved to hear him speak.

In the 1840s Johnson became a slaveholder at a "big auction in Greeneville." He did so after a slave named "Dolly," who was to be sold that day, came up to him and asked him to buy her and her brother Sam. Dolly's son William Andrew Johnson (who was born years later) recalled that his mother "…looked around the crowd of buyers before the auction started, and she saw Andrew Johnson and liked his looks. So she went up to him and asked him if he wouldn't buy her. He bid her in for five hundred dollars. And he bought my uncle, her brother, for five hundred forty dollars."

One thousand and forty dollars was a large sum of money at the time, more than a laborer would make in a year. Thus at some expense, Andrew Johnson became a slaveholder—at the request of the slaves he bought.

Thought to be Dolly, Johnson's slave

Sam Johnson, Dolly's brother

This was a tradition among East Tennessee emancipationists: buying slaves to keep them from being sold to a commercial plantation in the cotton states of the Deep South. Thus Johnson continued to further the cause of the East Tennessee emancipationist movement, even as he purchased slaves. He was building a solid record of working for emancipation. He had argued and voted in favor of emancipationist interests in the State Legislature. He had assisted his constituents in freeing their slaves by submitting their request to the state legislature that the freed slaves be allowed to remain in Tennessee.

In 1841, Johnson introduced a bill in the State Senate to make East Tennessee a separate state. This idea was then current among the East Tennessee emancipationists. They believed that once the region became a state they could vote to end slavery in the proposed state of East Tennessee, which was to be called "Frankland." "Frankland" meant the "Land of the Free," and once before had been considered as the name of a State of East Tennessee.

Johnson was growing in popularity with the voters, and his stand against the slaveholding aristocracy was a large part of the reason. He opposed slavery for moral reasons, but also for reasons of practical politics. He wanted to give political power to the working class instead of the wealthy aristocracy.

During these years, the town of Greeneville was slowly expanding. In 1842 Greeneville College opened a new campus on a hill at the northeast edge of town in a large, two-story square brick building with massive walls. The hill became known as "College Hill," and is today called "Circle Drive." Below College Hill was a musterground (where present-day Greeneville High School is located), which had been used for many years and marked the northeast edge of town. Another musterground, called the "Terrill Field," marked the southwest edge of town. The Terrill Field, later called the "Terry Field," eventually became the site of Crescent School.

The town covered ten or more blocks by the 1840s. The Dickson-Williams Mansion still had the elaborate porch of the pre-war photograph, and there were other mansions in town. The John Dickson home on Main Street was called "The Mansion"—a beautiful home with dark red brick and green shutters. These structures, with the three story William Dickson home on Main Street, and the brick Valentine Sevier home near the "Big Spring" gave the town the look and reputation of "aristocratic Greeneville." The population of Greeneville during the 1840s and 1850s was several hundred, and was nearing a thousand by the time of the Civil War of the 1860s.

The political leaders of "aristocratic Greeneville" were not an exclusive elite, however, and Andrew Johnson was accepted by them as a man of ability. From his earliest days in Greeneville he was allowed to attend and participate in student debates at Greeneville College even though he never enrolled at the school. Johnson studied the basics of reading and writing in his wife's schoolbooks, and he was introduced to higher education at Greeneville College.

The educational elite accepted Johnson readily, and in his early campaigns, so did the political elite. In his early campaigns he called himself a Whig, and could count the Whig leader Dr. Alexander Williams among his friends. Dr. Williams was the wealthiest man in the town and lived in the Dickson Williams Mansion.

After Johnson declared against state aid to an East Tennessee railroad, many of the Whigs turned against him, and he soon ceased to count Dr. Williams among his friends. By the mid-1840s, Johnson was calling Dr. Williams the "Grand Duke of Lick Creek," in reference to a large farm he owned near Lick Creek. Johnson had become a Democrat, and he remained a strong Democrat throughout a long and eventful political career. His speaking style was well developed by the 1840s. He used blunt, direct language with few practiced flourishes. He researched his issues and presented them forcefully. In debate he took and gave hard blows: verbal attacks on the opponent's character were common in Tennessee politics at the time. But after the debates, Johnson was always ready to shake hands with his opponents. When the elections are over, he believed, we are all Americans.

Chapter Two
Abolitionist in Disguise

Johnson's views on slavery are often misunderstood. In the years before the Civil War, he believed in the emancipation of slaves, which he understood as a process that would take years. When the idea of an immediate abolition of slavery by violence or disunion arose, Johnson opposed it, thus he was an emancipationist, but not an abolitionist.

By the 1840s however, Johnson's political opponents in Tennessee were accusing him of abolitionism. In a political newspaper, editor William G. Brownlow called Johnson an "Abolitionist in Disguise." Brownlow maintained that he was quoting a newspaper in Nashville.

Johnson's stands in favor of emancipation made the description seem true, but Johnson insisted he did not agree with the "abolitionists proper" who were advocating abolition of slavery by violence and disunion. And indeed some Northern abolitionists were beginning to advocate breaking the Union apart, leaving two nations, one slave and one free. The Northern abolitionists would thereby escape being associated with the evil of slaveholding. For Southern emancipationists this was the worst possible solution: it would leave them hopelessly in the minority in a slave-based Southern nation.

The problem was that slavery was recognized in the U.S. Constitution. Although the word "slavery" does not appear, the Constitution does refer to the slave as a "Person held to Service or Labour." The Constitution left decisions concerning persons "held to Service or Labour" to the state legislatures. This included the question of emancipating slaves. During Johnson's early career, emancipation was gradually working across the political landscape state by state. Gradual emancipation had ended slavery in many of the Northern states. New York passed its emancipation law in 1827, the year after Johnson arrived in Greeneville. New Jersey passed its gradual emancipation law in 1846, and in the 1860 census, eighteen people were still listed as slaves in New Jersey.

When the demand for immediate abolition of slavery by a law of the U.S. Congress arose, Johnson opposed it as unconstitutional. But he continued to favor emancipation, and he advanced the cause of freedom whenever he got a chance. There was a growing record of Johnson's opposition to the slaveholding aristocracy. His 1836 vote in favor of allowing the circulation of abolitionist literature was followed in 1839 by his presentation to the state legislature of an emancipation petition for two of his constituents, in which the petitioners asked that their freed slaves be allowed to remain in Tennessee. In December 1841, Johnson offered a bill to make East Tennessee a separate state. Separate statehood was then being discussed by the East Tennessee emancipationists. East Tennessee statehood was intended to get around the Tennessee Constitution of 1835, which said that the State Legislature could not emancipate slaves without the consent of the slaveholder. The new Constitution ended any immediate possibility of a law by the legislature ending slavery. If East Tennessee were a separate state, however, they would not be bound by the Tennessee Constitution of 1835.

Johnson advanced the cause of emancipation by any legal means available, but he opposed breaking the country into two or more smaller countries—no matter who was recommending it. He opposed disunion when advocated by the abolitionists, and later he would oppose disunion when advocated by the slaveholders. He did so because he believed the U.S. Constitution was the most perfect frame of government ever written, and that all social or economic problems could be worked out under its framework.

In 1842, Senator Johnson introduced a bill in the State Senate that would redistribute the existing Congressional Districts so that

East Tennessee—which had far fewer slaves than Middle and West Tennessee—would get one more representative in the U.S. House of Representatives. Johnson proposed to do this by basing the distribution of Tennessee's Congressional Representatives on the number of voters in each district, not the existing standard of Congressional Representation—the free population plus three fifths of the slaves. His opponents believed he was trying to get the representation of Tennessee and eventually the entire slaveholding South reduced. Johnson denied that this was his goal, but the accusations continued.

During Johnson's early years in Greeneville, free blacks could vote in Tennessee, but they lost the vote in the new Tennessee Constitution of 1835. Johnson accepted the blacks' loss of voting rights, but he pushed for a more democratic system of elections among white voters, opposing all property qualifications for voters. He believed that the common man was intelligent and well informed enough to vote. Johnson rarely if ever spoke of votes for women, which was not yet a major political issue. After the Civil War and the emancipation of slaves, Johnson began to advocate black voting with qualifications of property, education and military service, believing that the lack of education among the ex-slaves placed them in a different status from white voters.

During his time in the Tennessee legislature, from 1836 to 1843, Johnson pushed for education reform, especially giving more money to local schools. He also stood for economy in government and a strict accounting of public funds. In 1843 he was elected to the U.S. House of Representatives from the First District: that of the northeast corner of the state. The Second District had Knoxville as its center. Johnson served five terms as First District Congressman, from 1843 to 1853.

In an 1844 congressional speech in support of a resolution against receiving abolitionist petitions, Johnson agreed with Massachusetts Congressman John Qunicy Adams that emancipation was a proper goal of the political process, but Johnson argued against receiving abolitionist petitions because they advocated bloodshed and disunion if necessary to achieve emancipation.

In this speech Johnson said that blacks do not have talents equal to whites and thus should not have voting rights. This was a commonly held belief at the time because in slavery, blacks were not given an opportunity to show their abilities. They were usually given the hard, manual tasks of a farming economy, although a few slaves did become carpenters and skilled craftsmen. Overcoming this misconception was a long struggle for Johnson, as it was for most white Americans. Even in the 1840s, however, he was advocating emancipation as the proper goal of American politics.

During the winter of 1844-1845, Johnson's faction of the Democratic party held a series of political meetings in Jonesborough that were racially integrated. Parson Brownlow, a leading Whig, wrote in his newspaper that the Democrats "joined the <u>Negroes</u> of this town and county in an extensive Supper, and <u>Negro Dance</u>, at Chester's tavern." Brownlow noted that "one of the white orators addressed the company, and after fairly recognizing the negroes as an important part of the Democratic family, proceeded to advise them as to their future course...." Emancipation was gaining adherents among the Democrats of East Tennessee.

Shortly after this integrated Democratic Party meeting, Congressman Johnson, Democrat of Tennessee, spoke to the House of Representatives concerning the annexation of Texas. He favored annexation, and among the reasons he gave was that Texas would add enough land to the United States that the slaves could be emancipated without damaging the economy. Then, he said, "...the sable sons of Africa are to pass from bondage to freedom...."

Johnson believed in emancipation in its mildest form: gradual, planned emancipation, with the option of colonization of the freed slaves. He wanted this to be granted by slaveholders and state legislatures, believing that the national Congress had no power to free slaves. But the slave states of the Deep South were unlikely to pass emancipation. Besides emancipation by state legislatures and courts, there remained the possibility of a constitutional amendment, which requires a two-thirds majority in both houses of Congress, and ratification by three fourths of the state legislatures.

Johnson's answer to the impasse over how to end slavery was the Homestead Bill. He introduced this bill in 1846. It would provide a free 160-acre farm for anyone who would go to the western territories, build a homestead and farm the land for five years. Johnson wanted a nation of independent farmers who owned their own land. This was opposed by the Southern slaveholders because the most likely homesteaders of 160-acre farms were not slaveholders, but farmers who would work their own land without slaves. This would populate the West with free labor (that is, non-slave labor), and these territories would come into the Union as "free states," not as "slave states."

The homestead principle became the philosophy of a new political party, called the "Free Soil Party." While Johnson never joined the Free Soil Party, he often cooperated with them in day to day politics. Eventually the Free Soil Party was absorbed by the Republican Party, which was created in the mid-1850s.

In 1851, Congressman Johnson bought a new brick home on Main Street. The family—Andrew, Eliza, Martha, Charles, Mary and Robert—moved into the spacious home. Another son, Andrew Johnson Jr., was born there in 1852. He was called ""Frank" by the family, for reasons that remain obscure.

Johnson's Tennessee district, the First Congressional District, was redrawn in the early 1850s, and enough Whig counties were added to the district that Johnson was unlikely to win the next election. This kind of political maneuvering was called "Gerrymandering" a district, after Elbridge Gerry of Massachusetts, who had done such a thing early in American history. Johnson called the redrawn district a "Henrymander," after Gustavus Henry, a

**Andrew Johnson "Homestead" on Main Street,
his Greeneville home from the 1850s to his death**

political foe who led the movement to redraw the district. Johnson decided not to run in the redrawn district.

He was urged to run for Governor, and he did so in 1853. His opponent was Gustavus Henry, who had "Henrymandered" him out of his seat in Congress. Johnson's advocacy of emancipation was cited against him; his opponents called him an "abolitionist." An abolitionist society in New Jersey had included Johnson in a resolution of thanks, and this was cited against him. When he won the election, his opponents believed that his emancipationist ideas were the reason.

Johnson's Inaugural as Governor of Tennessee was held at the McKendree Church in Nashville, and his speech is remembered as the "Jacob's Ladder Speech." In the speech he compared democracy to Jacob's Ladder in the Bible. In the American system of government, he said, a person born poor could rise to whatever position his ability could take him: he could climb the ladder of success as high as his talents would allow. Johnson talked in religious as well as political terms throughout the speech, and it became the subject of many jokes. He was called a demagogue—someone who tries to trick the mass of people (the "demos") into following him. His opponents wondered how this uneducated man could make sense of such deep philosophical questions. But Johnson's basic conclusions were sound: American democracy was on the path to an increasing equality of opportunity for everyone.

As Governor, Johnson undertook to make the state government run efficiently, without having to borrow money. He was successful and became popular. He pushed for increased public funding for schools. An heroic act of personal bravery during his first term increased his popularity. A boarding house in which he was staying caught fire. Johnson escaped, leaving behind some clothes and money. Once away from the fire however, Johnson heard that a woman was still in the burning building. He went back into the building, through the flames, and led her to safety. His sound management of state finances, his advocacy of state aid for public schools, and his personal heroism made him popular, and he won reelection in 1855.

After two terms as Governor, he stood for the U.S. Senate. Senators in those days were chosen by the State Legislatures, and Johnson had great popularity among Democratic politicians for the victories he had won. Johnson was elected, and joined the Senate.

As Senator, Johnson returned to the issue of the Homestead Bill. He pushed for it in every way possible, and did not like to debate certain other issues. Debating slavery, he felt, was divisive and not likely to resolve anything. Slavery increasingly dominated the debates of Congress. The Homestead Bill finally passed both houses of Congress but was vetoed by President Buchanan.

**Andrew Johnson about the time he was
elected Tennessee Senator by the State Legislature**

The late 1850s were eventful years for Senator Johnson. He was in a train wreck and broke his right arm. The bone was badly set and troubled him for the rest of his life. The country was prosperous and Johnson's career was successful. His daughter Martha married David Trotter Patterson, and they purchased a farm near Henderson Mill. The Patterson home place became a place for Johnson to go for rest and privacy. The house was a large white frame house with a wide front porch. The Johnsons and Pattersons referred to the place as "home," and for a time Henderson Mill was called "Home." Eventually Henderson Mill became known as "Afton."

As the secession crisis grew, Johnson threw himself into the fight to save the Union. He had always believed that a broad-based suffrage in the South was the best way to end slavery. The word "suffrage" means "allowance," in the sense of Jesus when he said, "suffer the little children to come unto me"—that is, allow ("suffer") the little children. Thus the right of suffrage is the right to be allowed to vote. The mass of Southerners did not own slaves, and with the vote in their possession, the Southern people would see that it was in their interest to end the archaic, inhumane slave labor system. Johnson warned in a Senate speech in December 1860, that the Southern aristocrats planned to require a three-fourths majority vote to change the domestic institutions of a state—and that meant slavery.

On January 13, 1861, Johnson wrote his friend Sam Milligan of Greeneville a letter discussing the coming rebellion and war: "you now see that it is not guara[n]tees in reference to slavery they want: it is a go[vern]ment South so that they Can have the absolute Control of it in their own hands—And would erect today a monarchy if they had [it] in their power—I know what I say—It is not the free men of the north they are fearing most: but the free men of the South and now desire to have a go[vern]ment so organized as to put the institution of Slavry beyond the reach or vote of the nonslave holder at the ballot box."

Johnson was working to avoid the Civil War by ending slavery at the ballot box. But the secession of the Deep South was a fact by February 1861, and Tennessee was planning to have a vote on leaving the Union. Johnson used his influence, and fully 81% of East Tennessee voters voted against separation from the Union that February. The state as a whole was 55% against, and Johnson received the congratulations of many Tennesseans for his role in the victory.

At this time, a Tennessee abolitionist named Ezekial Birdseye wrote a letter to Senator Johnson, stating: "I congratulate you on the results of the late election in this state. Since I wrote you some weeks since, I have been in sev[e]ral counties of East Tennessee. I hardly heard but one opinion as to your course, all with a very rare exception approved it in the warmest terms. Not only in this state but in others particularly the Northern states speak of you with great respect as a statesman." That is how the avowed abolitionist, Ezekial Birdseye of Cocke County, viewed Andrew Johnson's role in Tennessee politics in 1861.

The states of the Deep South had already begun to secede by February 1861. The word "secede" means to withdraw from, and is related to the word "cede," which means to give to someone else. One of the major debates of the Civil War era was whether or not a state could secede, or withdraw, from the Union.

The politicians of the Deep South maintained that the states had voluntarily joined the Union and that they should be able voluntarily to withdraw. Northern politicians argued that the money from taxes and the lives of soldiers from all the country had been sacrificed in war to maintain the nation and that had created an indissoluble bond of nationhood.

Underlying this debate was the issue of slavery. Many in the North believed that the institution of slavery was an evil and must be ended. Those Southerners who agreed wanted emancipation to be gradual and by the action of state legislatures. This opinion was held widely in the border states, and by a few politicians such as Andrew Johnson. A larger number of Southern politicians, especially in the Deep South, believed that slavery was a good idea, allowing large commercial plantations to function without having to hire free laborers. Some of the slaveholders believed that they were introducing their African slaves to civilization and Christianity, thus were helping them.

The elite class slaveholders who believed that slavery helped the slave were Johnson's political opponents. They operated commercial slave plantations and lived in mansions, with ample free time and comfortable incomes. Their lifestyle was so comfortable that they convinced themselves that their civilization must be preserved, slavery and all. There were long-standing regional conflicts between the North and the South that gave the Southern independence movement plausibility—disputes over the tariff policy and the like.

When war came, many Southerners were prepared to defend Southern independence. In fact most of the Southern population supported the movement once the lines were drawn and armies were beginning to form. Yet most of the Southern foot soldiers were not slaveholders. They were the militia of the South, defending their homeland. The Deep South was controlled politically by a small elite of wealthy individuals, usually slaveholders, who made the decisions. This turned out to be a terrible mistake, because the elite decided for leaving the Union. Many Southern aristocrats insisted that the North would not try to force them back into the Union, and that if they tried, they would fail. In the end, this elite group destroyed themselves and much of Southern society as it then existed.

For Andrew Johnson the problem was easily solved: secession was illegal and therefore the Southern states could not withdraw from the Union. When Tennessee did withdraw from the Union in June 1861, Andrew Johnson remained in the U.S. Congress as Senator from Tennessee.

Fort Andy Johnson — During the Union occupation of Nashville (1862-65), the Capitol was transformed into a fortress. Fortunately, the artillery located there never had to be fired in battle.

Chapter Three
The Civil War

The Confederate States of America was proclaimed on February 18, 1861, with Jefferson Davis as President for a six-year term. The Confederates began to raise armed forces to resist any attempt by the national government to stop their movement toward independence. The Confederates seized Federal arsenals in their territory to provide arms for their troops. A few forts held out. Fort Sumter, on an island in the harbor of Charleston, South Carolina, was placed under siege by the Confederates.

On April 12, 1861, Confederate forces bombarded Fort Sumter, beginning the Civil War. The event was celebrated wildly in the streets of Charleston and throughout the Deep South.

After the attack on Fort Sumter, President Lincoln called for 75,000 volunteers to form an army to enforce the laws of the United States in the South, where many now claimed that Federal law no longer applied. The call for troops caused many Unionists in the border states, such as Tennessee and Virginia, to decide to leave the Union. They opposed secession but believed that states which had seceded should not be forced back into the Federal Union.

The terms "Federal" and "Confederate" show the philosophies of the competing sections. The Southerners wanted a "Confederation"—a loosely organized group of independent states. They had argued for years for "States Rights," and against control by the "Federal" Government. A "Federal" system implies an organization in which the central government controls the states, the form of government increasingly favored by many in the Northern states in the 1860s.

After Fort Sumter was taken by the Confederates, Tennessee Senator Andrew Johnson returned to East Tennessee and began to work against Tennessee leaving the Union and joining the Confederacy. A vote was scheduled for June 8, and Johnson toured upper East Tennessee speaking for "No Separation" as defined in the upcoming ballot. The debates were fiery, and Johnson was hanged in effigy at Tusculum College and shouted down in Jonesborough. The crowds in Elizabethton and Rogersville were friendly.

On June 8, 1861, the people of the state voted to separate from the Union, and Johnson began to make plans to leave the state. Most East Tennesseans were against secession. Greene County had voted 78% for remaining in the Union in the voting of June 8. A Unionist Convention was planned to be held in Greeneville beginning on June 17, but Johnson began receiving threats from secessionists and decided not to wait for the convention.

On June 12, 1861, Senator Johnson left Greeneville in a coach driven by Rev. John P. Holtsinger, minister of the Greeneville Cumberland Presbyterian Church. Two army officers were riding escort. The divided loyalties of Greeneville were visible as Senator Johnson rode through the streets of town. At the Greene County Courthouse, the American flag flew from the flagpole, even though the state had officially withdrawn from the Union by the recent vote. Across the street from the "Stars and Stripes" waving in the breeze, a sign was hanging from a frame hotel—"A. Johnson Traitor." The town was split between Union and Confederate sympathizers, with the rural areas of Greene County solidly Union.

Johnson had many supporters along the road to Kentucky, and he stopped and visited old friends on his way out of Tennessee. He stopped to see John Park, an abolitionist who had been with Johnson in the early Greeneville debating society. Johnson placed his hand on the head of Park's son James and told him to "do as your father has done: stand up for your country and never desert the 'Old Flag.'" At Bean Station a local Confederate official tried to call out the militia to arrest Johnson, but no one responded to the call. Bean Station (a site now under the waters of Cherokee Lake) was in those days a crossroads village where the road to Kentucky began. Johnson still had the support of the people: he passed peacefully through Bean Station and was on his way to Kentucky. Johnson and his companions heard gunfire in the distance as they rode through Cumberland Gap into Kentucky.

Senator Johnson spoke along the road through Kentucky, giving brief, passionate speeches with the theme: the "Hell born, Hell bound rebellion" has run us out of East Tennessee, but not for long. By the time he reached Cincinnati he was on horseback, with a small troop of cavalry as guard. They came into town riding hard—dust covered, with their horses lathered and panting. Johnson gave a short, hard-fighting speech and left the next day for Washington.

In Washington he met with President Abraham Lincoln and urged him to order a Federal invasion of East Tennessee. Johnson assured Lincoln that East Tennesseans remained loyal by a large majority. Johnson also pointed out that the railroad through East Tennessee supplied food and troops to Richmond, the capital of the Confederacy. Lincoln soon agreed, and Senator Johnson began to assist setting up underground networks in East Tennessee to prepare for an invasion. He was given the power to disburse money to underground groups in East Tennessee.

Many important military leaders including General George B. McClellan understood the advantage of the East Tennessee invasion—it would cut one of the two railroads that carried supplies to Richmond. Meetings began concerning the East Tennessee invasion. An East Tennessee civilian named Rev. William B. Carter met with General McClellan and President Abraham Lincoln. After two months of planning, Rev. Carter and a few Union military officers left the Federal military camps in Kentucky, bound for Tennessee. They were all in civilian clothes, which was a crime punishable by death for army officers. Rev. Carter was a civilian acting in a military operation in enemy territory: thus he was also subject to execution if captured.

On an October night, one of the Union officers who was assisting Rev. Carter, Captain Thomas Tipton, knocked on the door of Rev. Carter's home near Elizabethton, in Carter County, East Tennessee. Captain Tipton told the family he had a message from Rev. Carter and Senator Johnson. Tipton asked them to go get Daniel Stover, who was married to Johnson's daughter Mary, and bring him to the meeting.

Mary Johnson Stover

**Johnson's grandson, Andrew Johnson Stover,
with Johnson's slave, Florence. Andrew Johnson
Stover's parents were Dan and Mary Johnson Stover.**

Dan Stover soon came, and Captain Tipton told the group that the Federal government wanted volunteers to burn the railroad bridges on the Holston and Watauga Rivers. Stover immediately took the assignment and was sworn into the army. Johnson had brought his own family into the risky operation. The Unionist bridge burnings of 1861 were to prepare the way for a Federal invasion from Kentucky, but General William Tecumseh Sherman, Federal Commander in Kentucky, called off the invasion. When Senator Johnson heard the invasion was off, he mounted his horse and struggled through driving rain and bottomless mud to Federal headquarters to protest the decision. His efforts were in vain: the invasion was off.

The bridge burners did not know the invasion had been canceled, and on November 9, 1861, they attacked railroad bridges from Alabama to near the Virginia line. Several bridges were damaged. The Lick Creek bridge in Greene County was totally destroyed. When no invasion followed the Confederates struck back: thousands were arrested on suspicion, a few hundred were sent to prisons in the Deep South, and five were executed by hanging. Dan Stover fled with the others to the mountains. Stover joined the famed scout Dan Ellis, who was camping in the mountains. They lived the rest of the winter in cabins they built with their own hands. Other Johnson family members also went into hiding.

Robert Johnson

Senator Johnson's first attempt to advance Federal military power had failed disastrously. As a result, his son-in-law Dan Stover and son Robert were fugitives hiding in the woods and mountains—"in the bresh," as one East Tennessean wrote Johnson. Another son, Charles, also "stayed out" for a while but then came in and took the oath of allegiance to the Confederacy. Another Johnson son-in-law, Judge David Patterson, was arrested and threatened with prison before being released. Taking an oath of allegiance to a government which exists in fact—a *de facto* government—was legal in the Anglo-American legal tradition.

Many East Tennessee Unionists of military age began to hike overland to Kentucky and the Federal military camps. Men known as "pilots" guided small groups along the roads, trails and backwoods. They came by the thousands, in all kinds of weather, and several regiments were raised for the Federal army.

In December 1861, Senator Johnson joined the Joint Committee on the Conduct of the War, a committee of the U.S. Congress. The committee was formed to investigate Federal military failures. The committee was composed of members from both the House and Senate: thus they were a "Joint Committee." The committee was dominated by Radical Republicans, and Ohio Senator Ben Wade, a leading Radical, became chairman. The Radicals were in favor of an immediate invasion of the South, and harsh punishment for the rebels. Unfortunately for the Federal cause, they did not understand military affairs. The Radicals that controlled the Committee wanted General McClellan to march down to Richmond, attack the rebels and "bag" their army. The Southern armies were too efficient to be disposed of so easily.

As a member of the committee, Johnson tried to be fair to the subjects of their investigations. Johnson understood McClellan's commitment to an East Tennessee campaign, and they often agreed on military strategy. But Johnson soon had to resign from the committee to take a more dangerous and difficult mission at the request of President Lincoln: Johnson was appointed Military Governor of Tennessee.

The war in the East had been a series of Federal defeats, but in the West, a Federal army under General Ulysses Grant took the forts at the mouths of the Tennessee and Cumberland Rivers in February 1862. With steamboats and gunboats, the Federal troops quickly took Nashville, the capital of Tennessee. The Confederate Tennessee government fled first to Memphis, then to Chattanooga and into the Deep South. Confederate Tennessee had lasted less than a year.

President Lincoln appointed Senator Andrew Johnson as Military Governor of Tennessee on March 3, with the rank of Brigadier General. Johnson resigned from the Committee on the Conduct of the War and left for Nashville. He arrived at night, with no fan-fare. He was entering Middle Tennessee, which was a war zone. In speeches beginning soon after arriving, he told the people of Tennessee that the way to freedom was to re-establish a loyal state government and rejoin the United States of America.

An unusual and explosive situation was developing in Tennessee. East Tennessee, which favored the Union, remained under Confederate occupation. Middle and West Tennessee, which favored the Confederacy, was under Federal occupation. Johnson had taken on a most difficult task, and he soon realized it would be a long, hard struggle. The majority of the people in Middle and West Tennessee remained pro-Confederate during Johnson's months as Military Governor, and converts were slow in coming. He was offering Middle and West Tennesseans a civilian government under the U.S. Constitution, something they did not want.

Once he realized what he was facing, Military Governor Johnson instituted a harsh policy toward civilians who remained active supporters of the Confederacy. He would jail them, send them south, and confiscate their property whenever he felt it was justified, for example, to provide a hospital for wounded soldiers. He saw to the construction of fortifications around the city. The trenches and artillery positions were usually built with slave labor, and after the work was finished, the slaves were given their freedom.

As Military Governor, Johnson continued his contacts with Unionist civilians in Confederate East Tennessee who were willing to assist the Federal military. During Johnson's early months in Nashville, he was contacted by an agent of the management of the East Tennessee and Virginia Railroad and was told that the company would assist any Federal invasion by providing trains for the invaders. The E.T. & Va. Railroad ran from Bristol to Knoxville. A year later—in August and September 1863—the company would fulfill this promise by giving five trains to the invading Federals, despite repeated rebel orders to take the trains to Virginia.

During Johnson's first months as Military Governor, General George B. McClellan was removed from command of operations in the East. His replacement, General John Pope, was badly defeated at the Second Battle of Bull Run three weeks later, on August 29-30, 1862. His army fled in disorder from the battlefield. In the days that followed, many Federal officials feared Washington would fall to the Confederates.

The sudden series of Confederate successes in summer 1862 led to a general Confederate offensive: under General Robert E. Lee in the East and General Braxton Bragg in the West. Lee's victorious Army of Northern Virginia invaded Maryland that September. In the West, Bragg's Confederate Army of Tennessee marched into Kentucky. Maryland and Kentucky were loyal slave states: if both could be added to the Confederacy the balance of power would be altered.

As the Federal army prepared to fall back from Nashville to confront the invasion of Kentucky, Johnson demanded that an infantry brigade be left to garrison the city. Nashville was soon surrounded by Confederates, but Johnson would not allow talk of surrender. Nashville was cut off from supplies by rail, but the city did not fall. The capitol building became known as "Fort Andy Johnson." From the ramparts of "Fort Andy Johnson," the governor watched fights with raiding Confederate cavalry in the outskirts of town. There was never a full-scale Confederate attack on the city, but for a time, such an attack seemed likely.

In Washington just after the defeat of Federal General Pope, Lincoln again offered General McClellan command of the Army of the Potomac. Lincoln acted despite the loud protests of Radicals in the cabinet, many of whom had plotted to have McClellan removed. McClellan accepted; and within two weeks, he led the Army of the Potomac to victory in the battle of Antietam and drove the Confederates back into Virginia. The war now seemed a stalemate: neither side could successfully invade the other.

On September 22, 1862, Lincoln issued the preliminary Emancipation Proclamation. This document offered any of the Confederate states the opportunity to return to the Union with slavery still legal. There were still four slaves states who were loyal to the Union, and a fifth, West Virginia, joined during the war: they were not included in the Emancipation Proclamation. Nor was Tennessee, which was under Federal Military Government and thus not in rebellion. Lincoln believed that he had no power to proclaim freedom in the loyal states, because the power he claimed was a war emergency power. The preliminary Emancipation Proclamation warned that states that remained in rebellion after January 1, 1863, would have their slaves proclaimed free.

McClellan was removed from command in early November. His replacement, General Ambrose Burnside, was decisively defeated at Fredericksburg, Virginia, in December, and the North entered a winter of gloom. Lincoln was found in tears on occasion or ill with stomach cramps as he thought of the many thousands of battlefield casualties.

On January 1, 1863, Lincoln issued the Emancipation Proclamation. The document proclaimed freedom for slaves in states still in rebellion, and announced the acceptance of black recruits into the U.S. Army. The famous proclamation was strangely worded, giving freedom to slaves only in states still in rebellion, where Lincoln's proclamation could not be enforced. Slavery in the loyal slave states was not changed. There was, consequently, no immediate effect. But when a Union army advanced, all the slaves in the territory they entered were freed. Lincoln did this because he believed that he had the power to proclaim emancipation only as an emergency military measure.

Lincoln had resisted taking these steps because they were not widely popular in the North, and he feared it might break up the army. He also feared that the loyal slave states—Missouri, Kentucky, Maryland, Delaware and eventually West Virginia—might join the Confederates. Large battlefield losses helped convince Lincoln to proclaim emancipation as a war aim and to begin to enroll blacks in the army. Lincoln wrote Johnson that the manpower crisis facing the Federal army could best be met from the black population: "The colored population is the great available, and yet unavailed of, force, for restoring the Union."

Johnson began recruiting black troops, and when investigators came from the Federal government, he told them that three new regiments of black soldiers were ready and more would be raised. When asked how the blacks had done as soldiers, he responded: "They have performed much better than I expected. I was very agreeably disappointed. The Negro takes to discipline easier than white men, and there is more imitation about them than about white men. Then another thing: when the idea is in his mind, that the connection between him and his master is broken, and he has got white men to stand by him and give him encouragement, and a government which says, 'There is freedom before you—put down the enemies of the country; and if you desert, there is death behind you,' my impression is that, after a little while, he will fight. Of course, he must have some experience. The thing succeeded much better than I expected, and the recruiting is still going on."

Johnson's choice of words was strange: "I was very agreeably disappointed" meant that he had not expected them to do well—his expectations were "disappointed"—but that he was "agreeably" surprised at the good result. The blacks had made better soldiers than he had expected. Johnson's opinion of black people was changing, and he was beginning to see that in freedom they displayed more talents than he had foreseen.

As the Union army advanced the slaves who were freed by the Emancipation Proclamation began to collect in camps near the army.

Union General Lorenzo Thomas was sent to Tennessee to raise black regiments from among the refugee camps. General Thomas patiently but firmly insisted that the white soldiers accept the black soldiers into the army, and by the end of the war, General Thomas could claim success, in part, he said, because of the courage shown in battle by the black troops. General Lorenzo Thomas would play an important role in the Johnson Presidency.

Governor Johnson was moving toward immediate emancipation in his philosophy, and on August 8, 1863, he freed his personal slaves. The event was recalled by Will Johnson decades later: "One day Mrs. Johnson called us in and said we were free now. She said we were free to go or we could stay if we wanted to. We all stayed." Johnson's act of emancipation was taken by the black community of Tennessee as a promise that emancipation was coming. After Johnson fulfilled this promise in October 1864 by freeing the slaves of Tennessee, the "Eighth of August" began to be celebrated as Emancipation Day by blacks in parts of Tennessee and Kentucky.

Johnson gave other signs of his evolving view of race. On August 29, 1863, people gathered to celebrate the rumor that Fort Sumter had been captured by the Federals (the rumor turned out to be false). The crowd came to the Governor's house, and he came out to greet them. Johnson began speaking of emancipation. He said that "the heart of the masses of the people beat strongly for freedom, that the system of Negro slavery had proved baleful to the nation by arraying itself against the institutions and interests of the people, and that the time had clearly come when means should be devised for its total eradication from Tennessee." He stood for "immediate emancipation," but he would accept "gradual emancipation." He was for "emancipation at all events." Thus by August 1863, Andrew Johnson was calling for "immediate emancipation," and this was months before President Lincoln did the same.

That same August 1863, General Ambrose Burnside was in Kentucky planning a military campaign into East Tennessee, something Andrew Johnson had called for from the beginning of the war. Military Governor Johnson's allies within rebel-held East Tennessee contacted Burnside in his Kentucky camps. The invasion was launched, and from September 1 to 3, 1863, Burnside and the Army of the Ohio marched into Knoxville. The cavalry arrived on September 1, and found three complete trains at the E.T. & Va. Railroad Depot. The company President John R. Branner, the Chief Engineer J. B. Hoxie, and Oliver Temple, then a Knoxville attorney, were waiting at the depot to meet the Federal commander. With the advantage of these three trains and two more hidden up the line to Bristol, Burnside quickly conquered East Tennessee.

The Confederacy's only north-south railroad west of the mountains was now broken, and Federal General Rosecrans soon took Chattanooga, an important railroad junction in Southeast Tennessee. The Confederate Army of Tennessee attacked General Rosecrans and the Federal Army of the Cumberland at nearby Chickamauga on September 19 and 20. Rosecrans' troops were defeated, driven from the field and soon were besieged in Chattanooga. The Confederates began attempting to isolate and capture them. The Army of the Cumberland was the second largest Federal army: capturing it could bring Confederate victory in the war.

As part of the plan to isolate the Army of the Cumberland, a Confederate force of 2,000 under General John S. Williams advanced from Virginia and took positions east of Blue Springs (present-day Mosheim) in Greene County. Burnside's Army of the Ohio, 15,000 strong, advanced by rail and fought General Williams at Blue Springs on October 10, 1863. Williams' outnumbered Confederates held their line all day, then retreated through Greeneville during the night. There was a small battle at Rheatown on the 11th, and a wild, running chase to Virginia. Burnside was thus drawn away from Chattanooga, where the Federals remained under siege for another month. Burnside and the Army of the Ohio occupied Greeneville for a week or more, raising regiments from among the many Unionists. Thousands of Federal troops camped in Greeneville and Greene County, and recruiting went well. By early November they had returned to Knoxville, threatening the northern flank of the Confederates beseiging Chattanooga. The railroad had helped Burnside to perform these important maneuvers.

The Federal army in Chattanooga was reinforced from the West, and General Grant was put in command. In late November they drove the Confederates back into Georgia, thus ending the last chance the Confederacy had to win the war on the battlefield.

During these months of danger to the Union cause, Johnson was busy forming regiments and sending them to the front. In late November, the Federals regained the initiative, and East Tennessee appeared won. On November 23, 1863, Governor Johnson was interviewed by government investigators about managing the change from slavery to wage labor, with ex-slaves working as freemen for wages. Johnson said he was in favor of bringing the blacks into the wage-labor system as soon as possible. "My idea is, that with proper management, free labor can be made more profitable than slave, in a very few years. This will place the Negroes upon and within the great Democratic rule; it will unfetter industry, and if they have the talents and enterprise in them to rise, let them come."

Johnson's policy was to allow the blacks a chance to make it in society, and if they are successful—as he believed they would be—"let them come."

Johnson would repeat these themes in speeches in early 1864: that the blacks will be better workers in freedom than they had been in slavery, and their wages will rise as the worth of their labor rises. In this way they would join society as full citizens, and do it by their own efforts.

In January 1864, Johnson discussed the fate of the freed slaves with a Nashville crowd: "The God of Nature has endowed him with faculties that enable him to enjoy the result of his own labor. Political freedom means liberty to work, and at the same time enjoy the result of one's own labor, be he white or black, blue or gray, red or green." As the crowd began to laugh, Johnson shouted his conclusion into the tumult—"And if he can rise by his own energies, in the name of God, let him rise."

Johnson still believed that races had different talents, and that his own race was most gifted, but he said that the full talents of the freedmen could only be known in freedom. "There are degrees among white men; some are capable; some are not; some are industrious, others are not; but because we find inferiors among ourselves, shall every inferior man be assigned to slavery? If the negro is better fitted for the inferior condition of society, the laws of nature will assign him there. My own conviction is, that in less than five years after this question is settled upon the principle of hired labor, the negro's labor will be more productive than it ever was."

On April 12, 1864, the Knoxville-Greeneville Convention met again in Knoxville: it was the anniversary of the attack on Fort Sumter. Governor Johnson gave a speech in which he said: "The time has arrived when treason must be made odious, when traitors must be punished—impoverished; their property taken from them, whether it be their horses, their lands, or their negroes, and given to the innocent, the honest, the loyal upon whom the calamities of this unprovoked and wicked rebellion have fallen with such crushing weight." Then he added: "What has brought this war upon us? Let me answer in one word, let me speak it so loud that the deafest man in all this multitude can hear me—Slavery!" The crowd said: "That's so, that's God's truth."

Johnson ended his speech with a powerful statement: "Thank God for free speech and a free press, and the prospect of a free country! May God who is our Maker, and who will be our Judge, break every yoke, loose every shackle, open every prison door and let every bondsman, white and black go free!" This was followed by "loud applause."

The Knoxville Union Convention in April 1864 showed a division into Conservative and Radical Unionists: Johnson, who was advocating immediate emancipation, was among the Radicals.

In 1864 the Republican Party decided to rename itself the Union Party, in an attempt to foster national unity. Lincoln said little about the change, but he must have agreed with the idea. The Radical Republicans were making a terrible record of misguided interference in the war effort. The Radicals began to plan a third party effort in an attempt to prevent Lincoln's reelection, and Lincoln began to look for moderates and "War Democrats" as allies in the new Union Party. Lincoln feared that General George McClellan would be the Democratic nominee for president. Lincoln was willing to give General McClellan a command in the army, if he would not run for president. McClellan declined and became the Democratic Party candidate for President in the 1864 election.

As part of these political maneuvers, Andrew Johnson was offered the nomination to run as Vice President with President Lincoln. Even though Johnson was a Democrat, he accepted. He officially endorsed the Union Party goals, including complete emancipation. At the time, Johnson's hometown of Greeneville was still under Confederate control.

Earlier in 1864, Governor Johnson had created a cavalry brigade called the "Governor's Guard." They were created to take upper East Tennessee from the Confederates. Greeneville remained under Confederate control because once the Federals had taken Knoxville, the railroad into Virginia was broken. Upper East Tennessee was no longer strategically important. But it was important to Governor Johnson, and the Governor's Guard, under command of Johnson's friend Alvan Gillem, began a campaign into the area in August 1864, as the Governor himself was campaigning for the office of Vice President.

The Governor's Guard entered Greene County in late August and on the 23rd fought the Confederates at Blue Springs. The Confederates were outnumbered and began a fighting retreat. There was a running battle all the way through Greeneville, with the Confederates making brief fights along the way. The Federal pursuit was slowed, and the Confederates withdrew to the northeast.

The next week the Governor's Guard was involved in the Battle of Greeneville of September 3 and 4, 1864, in which the Confederate General John Hunt Morgan was killed. Battles between these fast moving cavalry brigades continued throughout the fall, and into 1865. When Johnson's hometown was occupied permanently by the Federals in December, the town showed the effects of several months fighting. Many houses had been battered with gunfire; the Cumberland Presbyterian Church had been hit with cannon, and the Greeneville College building had been damaged beyond repair. Grass grew tall in the downtown streets, with paths leading here and there. The rebels would raid the area from time to time, even into 1865, but Federal occupation had finally come. Tennessee had been unified under a Federal regime.

On October 24, 1864, Military Governor Andrew Johnson was called upon to speak by a torchlight procession of blacks at the capitol building in Nashville. He took the occasion to proclaim freedom for all the slaves of Tennessee: "I, Andrew Johnson, do hereby proclaim freedom, full, broad and unconditional to every man in Tennessee." Amid the cheering, Johnson continued: "I invoke the colored people to be orderly and law-abiding, but at the same time let them assert their rights, and if traitors and ruffians attack them, while in the discharge of their duties, let them defend themselves as all men have a right to do."

Johnson promised to break up the estates of the rebel leaders: their estates would be "divided into small farms and sold," the land would be sold to "small farmers...Nashville mechanics and tradesmen." And in fact many Tennessee Confederates would be convicted in post-war courts and charged fines so large that their lands had to be sold to pay the fines.

A famous exchange between the crowd and Johnson came toward the end of the speech. "Looking at this vast crowd of colored people," said Johnson, "and reflecting through what a storm of persecution and obloquy they are compelled to pass, I am almost induced to wish that, as in the days of old, a Moses might arise who should lead them safely to their promised land of freedom and happiness."

The crowd responded: "You are our Moses," and the "exclamation was caught up and cheered until the Capitol rung again." Johnson, like Moses of old, was reluctant to take on such a task: "God no doubt has prepared somewhere an instrument for the great work He designs to perform in behalf of this outraged people, and in due time your leader will come forth; your Moses will be revealed to you." The crowd replied: "We want no Moses but you!"

Johnson finally agreed: "Well, then, humble and unworthy as I am, if no other better shall be found, I will be your Moses, and lead you through the Red Sea of war and bondage, to a fairer future of liberty and peace. I speak now as one who feels the world is his country, and all who love equal rights his friends. I speak, too, as a citizen of Tennessee. I am here on my own soil, and here I mean to stay and fight this great battle of truth and justice to a triumphant end. Rebellion and slavery shall, by God's good help, no longer pollute our State. Loyal men, whether white or black, shall alone control her destinies; and when this strife in which we are all engaged is past, I trust, I know, we shall have a better state of things, and shall all rejoice that honest labor reaps the fruit of its own industry, and that every man has a fair chance in the race of life."

Johnson had attained the goal of the East Tennessee emancipationists, the goal Johnson had adopted in his early days in Greeneville and Greene County, and had furthered since his first term in the Tennessee legislature—freedom for the slave. A reporter who was present at the speech wrote that "it is impossible to describe the enthusiasm which followed these words.... The great throng moved back and forth in the intensity of emotion and shout after shout rent the air."

Lincoln and Johnson won the fall election; and that winter, Johnson began to work toward assembling a constitutional convention to make changes in the Tennessee Constitution including outlawing slavery forever. That would be much stronger law than the proclamation of a military governor. Johnson's final initiative as military governor was to convene a Constitutional Convention in Nashville in January 1865. The convention reconstituted the civil government of Tennessee, and passed a constitutional amendment ending slavery in the state. The question of voting rights for the freed slaves arose, and Johnson said that the question properly belonged with the state legislature. Within two years the vote would be given to blacks in Tennessee.

With the re-establishment of civil government, Johnson had fulfilled the mission Lincoln had given him in Tennessee. He was exhausted after these duties, and was ill from various ailments. He asked to be excused from the official inaugural ceremonies on March 4, but Lincoln and others urged him to come, and Johnson caught the train to Washington.

Johnson became Vice President on March 4, 1865. At his inaugural speech, the effects of a couple of glasses of brandy, taken by Johnson to relieve the symptoms of illness, gave rise to the accusation that he was drunk at his own inaugural. Johnson's illness was real, and he left Washington for the private residence of friends. He returned after a week or more of rest. He worked with Lincoln for about three weeks. In early April, the news began arriving of the surrenders of major Confederate armies. The war was ending and victory parties began.

The celebrating continued all week until the night of April 14, 1865. That night at Ford's Theater, President Lincoln was shot. He died the next day, making Johnson President of the United States. Johnson now faced the greatest challenge of his life. He was a Democrat taking office in a Republican administration; he was a Southerner taking office as U.S. President after a Southern rebellion costing over 600,000 soldiers' lives. And Johnson had before him all the questions of reconstruction of the Union and freedom for the slaves. Slavery was still legal in the United States, although all but Kentucky and Delaware had ended slavery by state action.

On the night of April 14, 1865, as Johnson paced the floor of his hotel room waiting for news of Lincoln's condition, he feared a spirit of revenge would arise, because people like to "kick the dead lion."

Chapter Four
President Johnson

Johnson had gone to sleep early on April 14, 1865, before the Lincolns arrived at Ford's Theater across town. In the night, Johnson was awakened by someone pounding on the door. It was the former Governor of Wisconsin Leonard J. Farwell. Governor Farwell told Johnson that President Lincoln had been shot. Johnson asked him to return to Lincoln's side and find out how seriously he was wounded. Johnson was left with a small military guard, and he began to ponder what it would mean to become president under these circumstances. He resolved to be fair to all, and to act in a way that a fair observer a hundred years later would conclude that his decisions had been right.

Lincoln died on April 15th and Johnson was sworn in the following day. He gave a brief speech in which he said that his lifetime goal had been to "ameliorate and alleviate the condition of the great mass of the American people." "Ameliorate" was a favorite word of Andrew Johnson's: his entire political career had been devoted to ameliorating—improving—the condition of the lower classes of America, and he promised to continue the policy as president.

Party politics would plague the Johnson administration, and the depth of political feeling around him became clear from the beginning of his presidency. Radical Republican Senator Ben Wade, with a group of his Radical supporters, met with Johnson the day after Lincoln died. Senator Wade said: "Johnson, we have faith in you. By the gods, there will be no trouble now in running the government."

The words "No trouble now" were spoken as Lincoln's corpse was being prepared to lie in state at the White House. Lincoln had been too conservative and too concerned with exact legal process for the Radicals. Radicals such as Ben Wade and Charles Sumner believed that President Johnson would support their plans without Lincoln's insistence on legal details. It took them a year or more to see that Johnson was as dedicated to exact legal process as Lincoln had been.

One of the first questions to arise in the Johnson Presidency was that of giving the freed slaves the vote. President Johnson encouraged the ex-Confederate states to give the vote to blacks who were literate or who owned property. He believed this would lead to universal voting rights as the freedmen took their places in society. In the North at the time, only five New England states and New York allowed the blacks to vote, and New York had restrictions similar to those Johnson was proposing to the South. At first the Radicals felt that Johnson agreed with them on voting. And indeed in the early months of the Johnson Presidency, many Radicals believed that the blacks should be given the vote over a period of years, as they acquired skills of citizenship, but not at once by an act of Congress.

Beginning in the summer of 1865, Frederick Douglass, the most prominent black leader of the age, began making speeches stating that the task of the anti-slavery movement is not completed until the blacks get the right to vote. Douglass was a forceful and persuasive speaker and soon many had been convinced. A movement for black suffrage began to grow. Johnson agreed in principle with universal suffrage, but he believed that constitutional standards should be adhered to, and that meant the state governments should write state voting laws.

Early in the Johnson Presidency, as the debate over voting rights was beginning, a trial was held in Washington for several people who were accused of conspiring with John Wilkes Booth to kill President Lincoln. Because the assassination had happened during a war and Lincoln was Commander in Chief, the War Department handled the assassination conspiracy trial.

Andrew Johnson, by Mathew Brady

The trial became one of the worst aspects of Secretary of War Edwin Stanton's entire career: a disgraceful mixture of perjured and coerced testimony. "Perjury" is lying under oath, and at least four perjurers were among the prosecution witnesses at the trial of the Lincoln assassination conspirators. In the end, four people were condemned to die. Only one of these, Lewis Payne, had done a violent act. It was never proven that Mary Surratt, who was also condemned to die, had knowledge of the murder plot. Mrs. Surratt ran the rooming house where the conspirators stayed, and her son John—who had escaped to Canada—had been an underground operative for the Confederates. John Surratt had conspired with John Wilkes Booth on many plots, but John Surratt was not associated in the murder plot.

A clemency request for Mary Surratt was written by a panel of officers from the trial jury, but President Johnson signed her death warrant without being told of the clemency request. Such were the intrigues of the Stanton War Department.

Johnson brought the ex-Confederate states back into the Union using a plan Lincoln was working on when he was killed. Lincoln intended a conciliatory peace, and when Secretary Stanton brought in a plan for military government of the Southern states to a cabinet meeting, Lincoln asked him to rework the plan using civilian governments. Johnson sent the revised plan to the ex-Confederate states to guide their way back into the Union. The pre-war voting population would select members of a constitutional convention: the convention would have to end slavery and repudiate all debts owed by the Confederate governments. They would then rejoin the Union.

Congressional Radicals were disappointed with this lenient plan and called it "Presidential Reconstruction." They were increasingly concerned that Johnson was being too conciliatory, just as they had been concerned about Lincoln.

Congress was out of session until December, and Presidential Reconstruction proceeded: most of the ex-Confederate states were restored to the Union. The only exception was Texas, where the process was not yet complete. When elections were held in the Southern states in fall 1865, only whites voted, and many ex-Confederate leaders were elected. Elections were won by Confederate Generals, Congressmen, Senators, and even the Confederate Vice-President, Alexander Stephens. Johnson feared this would ruin the conciliatory policy, and he wrote a friend in the Georgia military command that the vote showed "something like defiance, which is all out of place at this time." President Johnson also wrote the Governor of North Carolina: "The results of the recent elections in North Carolina have greatly damaged the prospects of the State in the restoration of its government relations."

In December 1865, the ex-Confederate Congressmen and Senators arrived in Washington, intending to take their seats in Congress. The sitting Congress voted not to allow any of them to be recognized as members. Even Unionist members of the House of Representatives from East Tennessee—people who had been accepted as Members of Congress throughout the war—were not allowed to take their places in Congress. Congressional Reconstruction had begun.

The South was continuing to show "something like defiance" by passing laws that came to be called the "Black Codes." These codes were designed to control the freed slaves. The people of the Deep South feared the freed slaves and wanted them controlled by special laws. To the people of the North, the "Black Codes" seemed like slavery was being reintroduced in a new form. The codes granted some rights, such as the right to marry, and the right to testify in court (but only in cases involving other blacks). But the black codes also denied other rights: the right to own land in some states, and the right to carry a gun.

Johnson did not say much about the "Black Codes," but allowed the Freedman's Bureau to deal with the problem. President Johnson continued to insist that the ex-slaves receive protection of their rights of person and property. The Black Codes were denounced and were soon modified or eliminated. President Johnson continued to try to bring all parties together, believing that if a peaceful way of life could be reestablished, the United States would return to economic prosperity, and jobs and homes would be found for everyone.

During the New Year's celebrations of 1866, President Johnson welcomed blacks to the White House, attempting, as always, to live his principles. He pointed out to Secretary of the Navy Gideon Welles that blacks were neither invited nor welcomed to the New Year's celebrations at Senator Charles Sumner's home, and Sumner was a leading Radical. Such subtle gestures were lost on the Radicals, who were intent on a conflict with Johnson. Senator Sumner had met with Johnson in late 1865 and concluded that he was opposed to the advancement of the freedmen, because he was opposed to military government of the ex-Confederate states.

As Johnson was trying to mediate the conflict between the post-war North and South, he was visited by Frederick Douglass and a black delegation. Johnson received them cordially, but would not agree to their central demand: immediate voting rights for the freed slaves. Johnson told them they had the same "end" but proposed to follow different "roads" to reach the goal. The promise of full voting rights someday did not satisfy Douglass, who turned to leave and said to the delegation: "He sends us to the people and we go to the people!" Johnson heard the remark and said, "Yes Sir, I believe the people will always do what is right!"

Johnson was angry at the persistence of Douglass, who had reargued every point and would not be denied. After the delegation left, Johnson reportedly went into a private office and cursed and used a racial epithet. Perhaps he did: Johnson had a temper. But he had recognized in Frederick Douglass a forceful leader, and a little over a year later, Johnson would offer Douglass a high position in the administration.

Johnson's conflicts with Congress increased in 1866 as he vetoed important legislation, including a new Freedman's Bureau Bill and a Civil Rights Bill. He always gave constitutional reasons for the vetoes, and the bills did contain some provisions of questionable constitutionality: for example, military trials for civilians accused of ordinary crimes to be held where civil courts were open. But Congress was dealing with a difficult situation, where white juries in the South were freeing white defendants accused of crimes against blacks. Johnson did not want that solution either: he refused, in one Georgia case, to grant a pardon to a white man sentenced to hang for killing a black woman. Johnson felt that the regular working of the civilian court would eventually handle such cases fairly.

In later months, Johnson learned of criminal conspiracies being conducted by some of his political opponents among the Radicals. Congressmen Ben Butler and James Ashley were reportedly trying to convince certain prisoners in the Washington D.C. jail to testify against Johnson. The charge they were concocting was that Andrew Johnson was part of the conspiracy to kill Abraham Lincoln.

Throughout 1866 the confrontation between Johnson and Congress grew. Johnson insisted that the ordinary process of law, under the Constitution, was sufficient to bring the country back into a peaceful and prosperous Union. He believed that many problems that seemed impossible to solve would work out in the long run. The Congressional Radicals believed that the South must be treated as conquered territory: the economic system of the South had to be rebuilt with Northern money and know-how, and the social and political system had to be restructured, with careful regard to the fate of the freedmen.

This difference was the essence of the veto battles of 1866. Johnson vetoed the Freedman's Bureau Bill in February because the bill contained unconstitutional powers, such as the denial of trial by jury. His veto was sustained. He vetoed the Civil Rights Bill because he believed it was unnecessary and unconstitutional. This veto was overridden. In July another, somewhat milder, Freedman's Bureau Bill was passed, vetoed by the President and passed over his veto by Congress.

By late summer 1866 the conflicts between the President and Congress were becoming the central issue of the coming Congressional elections. As the passion of an hotly contested election mounted, Johnson was invited to help dedicate a statue in Chicago to Stephen Douglas, a Democratic Party leader who had died a few years before. Johnson took the opportunity of the train ride to Chicago to engage in a speaking tour he called "The Swing Around the Circle." It would be a disaster.

Johnson's train first went through New York, long a Democratic state. There, he was well received. But when the tour reached Ohio, people in the audiences began to argue with him. He answered with impassioned argument. Arguing with the crowd was politics, Tennessee style, but Northern politicians, including most allies of Johnson, thought it was undignified. When people began to see that Johnson was going to speak at every stop, Radical Republican politicians made sure there were people waiting, prepared to shout questions and argue the Radical case. By the end of the tour people were hollering "Shut Up!" and "We want to hear Grant."

Johnson's party lost in the Congressional elections that year. The Radical victory was overwhelming, creating a two-thirds majority in both houses of Congress. This was important because a two-thirds majority in both houses of Congress was necessary to override a presidential veto. Thus the 40th Congress would be "veto proof."

Johnson believed that Radicalism was more interested in taking Southern property than in advancing black civil rights. He fought the Radicals' schemes where he felt justified. When Stanton and the War Department tried to confiscate the East Tennessee and Virginia Railroad, Johnson intervened and halted proceedings. He knew that the company management had helped the Union cause on numerous occasions. They had remained in Confederate East Tennessee operating the railroad and secretly supporting the Federal cause. Johnson also stopped the confiscation of church property in Nashville. Stanton was going to confiscate a Methodist church and its property because the Southern Methodist church had supported the Confederacy. That was not enough for Johnson, who believed that specific people and institutions had to be convicted of specific crimes before their property could be taken. The attitude of Secretary Stanton was that all who lived in the South were rebels unless they could prove otherwise, and that their testimonies to the contrary were all lies and tricks.

Many Southern Unionists had helped the Federal army but had kept no records of their efforts. Their property was to be confiscated along with that of the dedicated Confederate. Tennessee was exempt from the most extreme of these measures, because the state had fallen to the Union soon after the war began. Yet even in Tennessee, many ex-Confederates lost their land in the courts, where they were sued for trespassing and theft during Confederate requisitions. Murder and treason cases were also brought. Fines of thousands of dollars were imposed on those convicted. The area was drained of cash, and many of those found guilty had to sell their farms and homes and move away.

Radical demands increased, and became increasingly extreme. At first the Radicals advocated the extension of voting rights to blacks in the South, but soon they added taking the vote from the whites of the South. This was to be done because the whites had participated in rebellion. This policy was considered during the war, but was opposed by Lincoln as unjust and unwise. President Johnson issued his general amnesty in May 1865, pardoning those who had participated in the rebellion except for certain acts. Thus after May 1865, the policy of denying rights that had been restored to the ex-rebels was also illegal. None of this mattered to the 40th Congress.

The Radical 40th Congress convened in March 1867. The prior Congress had been almost as Radical, and the two Congresses merged without taking a break. The 40th Congress took up the bills being written and soon produced the First Reconstruction Bill, embodying the principle of black voting coupled with a loss of voting rights of whites who had participated in the rebellion.

These ideas had been debated in the president's cabinet early in 1867 when a bill to reorganize the government of Washington D.C. came before them. The bill would enfranchise the blacks and disfranchise the ex-Confederates, and the only cabinet member to support the principle was Secretary of War Edwin Stanton. By early 1867, Edwin Stanton was functioning as a spy within the Johnson cabinet for the Congressional Radicals, and Stanton was secretly helping the Radicals write laws that would take powers away from President Johnson. Cabinet member Gideon Welles warned Johnson that Stanton was conspiring with the Radicals, but Johnson had no proof and decided not to confront Stanton with the charge.

Chapter Five
Political War

Several Reconstruction Acts were passed, beginning in March 1867: each law increased the powers of the military government of the South. Johnson vetoed them all, and all were passed over his veto. When Johnson lost each veto fight, he attempted to enforce the law as the Attorney General interpreted it. The Congress would then pass another law overturning the Attorney General's interpretation. In that way a number of Reconstruction Acts were written, all tightening the military government of the South.

Johnson was not against the social and political progress of the blacks, but he wanted it done under constitutional laws, not by emergency laws and military government. Other laws were passed to restrict the powers of the president. The Tenure of Office Act made the removal of a cabinet member subject to the assent of the Senate for the first time in U.S. history. A Military Appropriations bill was passed with a passage stating that the president could not communicate directly with the army, a clear presidential right and duty under the Constitution.

Johnson tried to be conciliatory with the Radicals. During the summer of 1867 he offered Frederick Douglass the position as head of the Freedman's Bureau. Douglass was the most prominent black leader of the age, and was a passionate advocate of full citizenship including voting rights for blacks. The Freedman's Bureau was the government agency that had been created to oversee the transition from slavery to freedom. With Douglass as Bureau head, there would only have been one choice—full civil rights for the freedmen. Douglass refused to accept the position.

Despite these efforts, the conflict of the President with Congress increased. Johnson discovered that Secretary Stanton had written the clause of the Military Appropriations Bill that took from the President the right to give direct orders to members of the military. This Presidential right was granted in the Constitution, where the President was made Commander-in-Chief of the armed forces of the nation.

On August 5, 1867, President Johnson received information in the mail from Sandford Conover, one of the perjurers in the Lincoln assassination trial. Conover had been convicted of a different perjury while he was employed by the War Department. Conover was in jail at the time, but he wrote President Johnson that he was willing to testify that Congressmen Ben Butler and James Ashley had urged him falsely to accuse Johnson of conspiring to murder Lincoln. Johnson had heard of this plot before, but here was proof from one of those involved.

By the same mail, Johnson received a package from the War Department containing the Death Warrants he had signed in the Lincoln assassination trial during 1865. The petition for clemency for Mary Surratt, which Johnson was seeing for the first time in 1867, was attached to the warrants. He realized that he could not discover the whole truth about criminal conspiracies as dark as these which were appearing in the working papers of the War Department, but he knew who had the ultimate responsibility for them: the Secretary of War Edwin Stanton. Stanton's War Department had found and employed Conover and his coconspirators in perjury. The War Department had worked with these people for months after their perjuries began to be exposed in the newspapers.

The same day Johnson received this mail, he sent a note asking Secretary Stanton to resign. Stanton replied that he would not resign. Johnson approached General Grant and asked him to take the job of Secretary of War on a temporary basis. Grant agreed. When Stanton heard that Grant had agreed, Stanton resigned, and Grant became Secretary of War *ad interim*.

As these events were transpiring, Johnson was attempting to get Frederick Douglass to accept the position as head of the Freedman's Bureau. His first refusal came on August 12, the same day that Stanton stepped down as Secretary of War. And Johnson continued to urge (through a mutual friend) that Douglass accept the position. The final refusal of Douglass came on August 18.

Four days later, on August 22, President Johnson gave an interview to a newspaper reporter and was asked how he wanted the Reconstruction Acts to be enforced. Johnson said he "desired a fair registration of all qualified voters without regard to race or color. He did not wish to give any advantage to the white men, but much less was he disposed to make them the slaves to the negroes. Where the negroes had the majority, as in South Carolina, he wished them to exercise the power; where the white vote was in the majority, as in Texas, he desired that white majority to control. He wanted only the law to be fairly executed with equal chances to all."

When Congress reconvened, partisan warfare began at once. Since January the Judiciary Committee of the House of Representatives had been investigating President Johnson in an attempt to find some legal charge on which to base Articles of Impeachment. There is very little in the report of this Congressional investigation about the civil rights of the freedmen. The investigation was all about Johnson's leniency with the ex-rebels—and especially his leniency in allowing Southern property to be returned to ex-rebels. He believed that the various shades of loyalty—from Southern Unionist to undecided to committed rebel—made leniency the only just policy. Ex-rebels should be punished, Johnson believed, only if specific crimes were proven against them.

The Judiciary Committee drew up Articles of Impeachment and presented them to the entire House of Representatives in late fall 1867. The first article concerned Johnson's handling of Southern railroads, and the records of the committee show that the East Tennessee and Virginia Railroad was prominent in their hearings.

The year before, President Johnson had stopped Secretary of War Stanton from confiscating the company and its equipment. Johnson apparently did not explain himself, acting as he was from knowledge of wartime military secrets—the E.T. & Va.'s assistance to the 1863 Federal invasion of East Tennessee. There was nothing in the Articles that even came close to the "high crimes and misdemeanors" given in the Constitution as the standard for conviction in impeachment cases. There were complaints of too many vetoes and too many pardons, but nothing of substance, and the Articles were quickly voted down.

President Johnson's Third Annual Message was a plea to Congress not to impose on the defeated South the policy of blacks voting and whites not voting. Such policy was sure to foster racial conflict, he said, but the Congress refused to heed the warning.

Johnson's view of the race question was constantly, slowly evolving. On December 31, 1867, he gave an interview spelling out his current thinking. He said that he "had predicted the abolition of slavery and the advancement of the negro race to a condition of happiness and freedom, and had spoken of a time not far distant when distinctions, based on the color of a man's skin, would be unknown in this country."

When Congress returned in January 1868, the Senate quickly voted to return Stanton to the office of Secretary of War.

Stanton took the office. The Radicals were looking for something—anything—to use to impeach and remove Johnson as President. When a disagreement arose in the Cabinet between Johnson and General Grant, the Congress considered impeachment charges, but did not proceed. The disagreement concerned a promise Grant had made to return the keys and papers of the War Department to Johnson. After the Senate voted to return Edwin Stanton to office, Grant was warned that it would be illegal not to give the material to Stanton, so Grant gave the keys and papers to Stanton. Johnson accused Grant of not keeping his word, which infuriated him. They never spoke again.

By February, Johnson had determined to fire Stanton. After considering a number of replacements, Johnson chose General Lorenzo Thomas to replace Secretary Stanton. General Thomas had worked closely with Johnson in Tennessee during the Civil War in raising black regiments and finding work for the freed slaves. General Thomas was experienced in successfully combating race prejudice in the U.S. Army, and President Johnson called him "right-minded."

The firing of Stanton brought a vote on impeachment in the House of Representatives. The House voted to impeach Johnson before a list of specific charges was produced. To "impeach" is to "accuse," and after accusing Johnson, the House had to produce articles of impeachment and present them to the Senate for trial. Having accused Johnson of crimes, the House set out to find some actual crime to accuse him of committing.

The articles of impeachment they produced were extremely weak. Edwin Stanton was not covered by the Tenure of Office Act because he had been appointed by Lincoln, and the law specifically stated that the act only covered persons appointed by a president and for one month after the president leaves office. Lincoln had been killed in 1865 and had been out of office for three years. In addition, in spring 1868 as the impeachment trial began, Stanton still held the office of Secretary of War. He had refused to be fired, had refused to leave the building and was living in his office at the War Department, surrounded by friends and supporters. Once Stanton refused to give up the office, Johnson did not send troops to remove him. The War Department mail continued to be delivered to the War Department and to Secretary Stanton, although Johnson could easily have stopped the mail from being delivered. Thus Stanton had not been removed from office, which was the subject of the first eight Articles of Impeachment of 1868.

The weakness of the eight Tenure of Office articles was soon realized and three additional articles were written. Article Nine concerned a meeting between President Johnson and General Emory in which Johnson had stated his objections to the law removing his right to give direct orders to the military. Article Ten alleged that some of Johnson's speeches were so inflammatory as to be impeachable offenses. Article Eleven was written by Thad Stevens, an elderly congressman who hated Johnson and the Southern states in equal measure. The eleventh article is strangely worded, but it is the only article to mention an alleged attempt by Johnson to subvert the working of the Reconstruction Acts. General Lorenzo Thomas was named in several of the articles as Johnson's co-conspirator in the attempt to remove Stanton.

The trial lasted several weeks, and the evidence was weak. Official papers were presented showing that Johnson had attempted to remove Stanton from office. These and other documents presented had been made public long before. Some of Johnson's speeches were entered into evidence, as if the First Amendment did not guarantee free speech to the President as well as to other Americans.

Johnson's attorneys effectively refuted the charges. Some of his attorneys reminded the Senate of how bravely Johnson had fought for the Union during the war. He had left the safety of Washington and gone into a war zone in Middle Tennessee in 1862 at the request of President Lincoln. "I have often thought," said William Groesbeck, one of Johnson's attorneys, "that those who dwelt at the north, safely distant from the collisions and strife of the war, knew but little of its actual, trying dangers. We who lived on the border know more. Our horizon was always red with its flame; and it sometimes burned so near us that we could feel its heat upon the outstretched hand. But he was wanted for greater peril, and went into the very furnace of the war, and there served his country long and well. Who of you have done more? Not one."

The weakness of the impeachment case inspired seven Republicans, some of them Radicals, to follow their oath to do impartial justice rather than the desires of their political party. With these seven and all the Senate Democrats, Johnson was acquitted by one vote. These seven Republican "recusants"—those who would not submit to authority—included Lyman Trumbell, one of the leaders of the party, and Edmund Ross, a Radical from Kansas. None of the seven were ever elected to office again. Ross realized that his political career was probably over, being a Senator from Radical Kansas. But he considered the not guilty vote a necessity given his oath to do impartial justice. The Constitution requires a two-thirds majority to convict in an impeachment case, and the vote was 35 to 19 in favor of conviction: one vote short of the required two-thirds majority.

After Impeachment, Johnson continued to conduct his office as he had done. With Lorenzo Thomas in the War Department, the department worked efficiently and a riot in New Orleans was stopped before it began. In his final months in office, Johnson sought reconciliation with everyone, even his strongest opponents. It was Johnson's way: a hard political fight, with a handshake at the end. During the holiday season of 1868-1869, he was having a reception at the White House. Long lines of visitors were waiting to greet him. Glancing down around the room, he noticed that Ben Butler was coming down the reception line. Butler was one of those who had plotted falsely to accuse him of the murder of Lincoln. Butler had been the leader of the House Impeachment team, who presented the case to the Senate in harsh and insulting terms. Yet Johnson was cordial, they shook hands and greeted each other.

President-elect Grant was less cordial. He let it be known that he would not speak to Johnson and would not ride in the same carriage with him to the Inaugural. Johnson remained at the White House until his term expired at noon, said his good-byes, got in a carriage and left. President Grant arrived at the White House a half-hour later, and the Radicals had taken control of all three branches of the government.

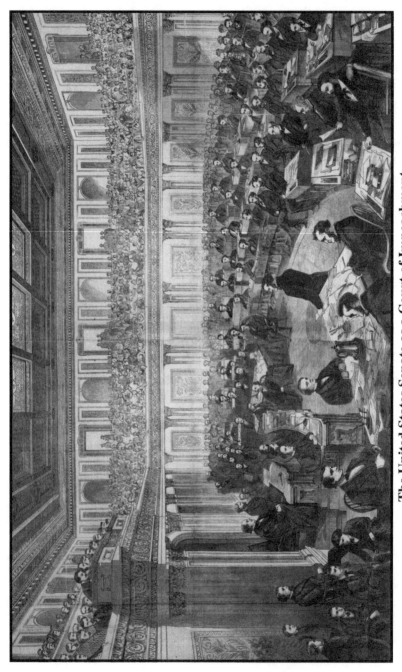

**The United States Senate as a Court of Impeachment
for the trial of Andrew Johnson, sketched by Theodore R. Davis**

Johnson, now ex-President, took the train home to Tennessee, and all along the line there were crowds of supporters and calls for him to speak. After all he had been through and had been accused of there were still many "Andy" Johnson supporters in the country.

Radical Reconstruction failed, as Johnson had predicted. The laws passed by the 40th Congress used the freedmen, in effect, as a means of punishing the ex-Confederates. The former slaves were given the vote, and the vote was widely withheld from the former Confederate soldiers. Some 200,000 Southern whites were disfranchised: enough to sway elections to the Republicans. Peace between the races could scarcely be expected from such unconstitutional and unwise laws.

Johnson believed in emancipation, and with freedom, he had insisted on maintaining the personal and property rights of the blacks. He wanted the literate and property-owning blacks to be given the vote immediately, and he expected that suffrage rights would be extended to all blacks in the near future.

Politics were passionate during these years, and there were many plots against Johnson while he was president. Officers of the government hired people who arranged with dishonorable men to tell the lie that Johnson was involved in the plot to assassinate President Lincoln. During these partisan wars, Johnson had remained calm, carefully conducting the government and letting the Radicals do the plotting. He was confident because his policy was that of Lincoln—moderation and conciliation between the North and South and between the races.

President Andrew Johnson Quotes

"There are no good laws
but such as repeal other laws."
Andrew Johnson, 1836

"Thank God for free speech and a free press,
and the prospect of a free country! May God
who is our Maker, and who will be our Judge,
break every yoke, loose every shackle, open
every prison door and let every bondsman,
white and black go free!"
Andrew Johnson, April 1864

"I, Andrew Johnson, do hereby proclaim
freedom, full, broad and unconditional,
to every man in Tennessee."
Andrew Johnson, October 1864

"I have long labored to ameliorate and
alleviate the condition of the great mass
of the American people. Toil, and an
honest advocacy of the great principle
of free government, have been my lot.
The duties have been mine—the
consequences are God's."
Andrew Johnson, April 1865

Chapter Six
Ex-President and Senator Johnson

When the ex-President reached Greeneville on the train-ride home, he was welcomed warmly by his old friends. He settled into his home on Main Street, and soon undertook a speaking tour of Tennessee, defending his presidency and the policies he had pursued. All the years of public speaking had honed his skills, and these speeches are marvels of concise, clear expression. On the subject of voting rights for blacks, he noted that he had been accused of favoring the policy in 1865 when he sent the Provisional Governors of the ex-Confederate States telegrams suggesting that the states grant blacks voting rights subject to literacy and property qualifications. Now, he said, he was being accused of opposing black suffrage: "Where's the proof of it? When I suggested that the State of Tennessee and others should go as far in one year as other States had gone in fifty years, it was a great advance."

In April, Johnson was on tour when he heard that his son Robert had died suddenly in Greeneville. Robert Johnson was given a "big Masonic funeral." He had been a State Representative and Colonel of the First Tennessee Cavalry, but he had suffered from various physical ailments including congestion of the lungs, probably tuberculosis. As a young man, he began taking opiates (which were legal at the time) and drinking

Robert Johnson

alcohol for these ailments. On April 22, 1869, he died in bed, after an overdose of laudanum, an opiate.

In his grief, Andrew Johnson retired to his Greeneville home for a time. Whenever he was home, Johnson liked to walk in the woods in the hills west of his home. His home on Main Street was considered the western edge of town, and there were few houses beyond nearby Brown's Hill. Johnson was often seen with a young black boy, probably Will, walking these hills. Will said of Johnson that "after he came back from Washington I was with him all the time." Sam also accompanied Johnson on these walks.

Some of the property in this woodland belonged to the ex-President, for example, the tall "Signal Hill," where Civil War signaling stations had been established. To the northwest, near the musterground known as the Terrill Field, was the road to town and the church and Freedman's School that Johnson had helped establish in 1867 by donating the land.

In summer 1869, Johnson began trying to find his pre-war personal papers, which had been taken in 1864 by some of General Longstreet's Confederates, who were then occupying the area. Johnson wrote to Longstreet and one of his staff officers, but they could give little information about what had happened to the papers. In 1864 the Greeneville Confederates had been given the papers, and they were carefully preserved throughout the war years. Confederate Major James H. Robinson and William M. Lowry, a civilian, were both in Greeneville at the time, and they corresponded with Johnson during 1869. Many of his pre-war papers were recovered as a consequence.

The Greeneville Confederates had taken steps to preserve Johnson's papers, which must have confirmed his belief that the conciliatory policy was the correct one. The patterns of loyalties and personal friendships were too complex to sort out, and the only way to keep from punishing innocent people and wartime friends was to punish only those found guilty of specific crimes. That had been

Johnson's policy throughout his presidency, and for it he had endured the wrath of the Radicals.

Johnson's desire to heal the wounds of war was shown in many ways. A young attorney named Elbert C. Reeves had settled in Greeneville after the war. Although Reeves had served as a Confederate Colonel, Andrew Johnson walked into his office one day, engaged him in a friendly conversation, and soon hired him as a private secretary.

Johnson remained open to reconciliation with his former enemies, but he opposed some ex-Confederates taking political office. In 1872 there was an election for the U.S. House of Representatives. The position was an office that no longer exists: "Congressman at Large." The election of 1872 was a state-wide contest. When the Democrats nominated an ex-Confederate general, Johnson entered the race as an independent. Johnson was a lifelong Democrat, and he split the Democratic vote, which allowed the election of Republican Horace Maynard, a wartime Unionist. As President, Johnson had risked his political career to preserve the rights of the ex-Confederates, yet in 1872 he entered a political contest he was sure to lose in order to split the Democratic vote and keep an ex-Confederate from winning. He wanted the ex-rebels to have their civil rights, but he did not want them running the government.

In interviews and speeches in his last years, Johnson justified his course as an attempt to restore American society. His outlook was religious: reconciliation of the country's various groups was his goal. Although he never joined a church, he gave to churches and attended meetings throughout his life. He defended religion and various Christian denominations in minor pamphlets and speeches.

This religious outlook was in his mind as he lay ill with Cholera in 1873, possibly dying. He wrote: "I have performed my duty to my God, my country and my family. I have nothing to fear. Approaching death to me is the mere shadow of God's protecting wing. Here I will rest in quiet and peace beyond the reach of calumny's poisoned shaft—the influence of envy and jealous enemies, where Treason and Traitors in state, back sliders and hypocrites in church can have no place—where the great fact will be realized <u>that</u> GOD IS TRUTH and <u>gratitude</u>, the <u>highest atribute of man</u>.

Adieu--Sic iter ad astra. Such is the way to the stars or immortality.

Written before leaving on Sunday eving while the cholera was raging in its most violent form."

Johnson was taken to the Patterson home near Henderson Mill, and within a few weeks was beginning to recover. He had almost died, and his total recovery was long and slow.

Johnson's good relations with his ex-slaves were maintained in his final years. He let Dolly and her family live in the Tailor Shop building, and she lived there until her death long after Andrew Johnson had died. Will recalled being Johnson's constant companion: "I slept right in the same room with him." When asked in 1937 by a journalist if "he wasn't better off when Andrew Johnson owned him," Will answered: "Yes, we were mighty well off then. But any man would rather be free than be a slave." Johnson's ex-slave Sam had written him in 1867, at the height of President Johnson's conflict with the Congress: "I am getting along as well as usual and have not changed any in Politics still being for you as much as ever. I would like to see you all very much."

Johnson was elected to the U.S. Senate in 1874, and he took his seat in 1875. During the session of spring 1875, President Grant asked Congress to confirm his decision to return General Phil Sheridan to the office of Military Governor of the district of Louisiana and Texas. Johnson opposed the idea. While he was President, he had removed Sheridan as Military Governor of the same district for corruption and for making large-scale removals of elected officials in those states, including the governors of the two states. In Johnson's 1875 Senate speech he warned that the Republicans would turn the anti-democratic strategies they had perfected in the Reconstruction South against the whole nation. The following year, 1876, was the year of the Hayes-Tilden Presidential election, in which a Republican candidate with a minority of votes became president after months of deals and bargains.

Back in Greeneville after his first session in the Senate, Johnson enjoyed a few months of rest. He had severe physical ailments: his broken arm had never healed properly. Will Johnson recalled, "He was paralyzed on one side. He would reach over with his good arm and take hold of his wrist and say, 'Is that your hand, William?' And I'd say, 'No, Mr. Andrew, that's your own hand.'" His right hand had lost all feeling.

In July 1875, Johnson decided to visit his daughter Mary Stover Brown in Carter County. After the death of Col. Dan Stover, Mary had married William Brown of Greeneville, but they continued to live in Carter County at the Stover family home.

On the train ride to Carter County, Johnson fell into conversation with a former Confederate officer named William McElwee. Johnson reviewed his own past political career. He said that he now believed Mary Surratt was innocent and had been put to death illegally by Stanton—a ghastly crime that had haunted Stanton until he lost his mind and committed suicide. Johnson recalled getting word of Lincoln's death and thinking of all the problems ahead and concluding that he must act in a way that a fair person a hundred years later would conclude that Johnson had "done the right thing."

He arrived by buggy at the small two-story frame Stover homeplace in Carter County. Mary Stover Brown lived in the home with her daughter Lillie. After a pleasant meal Johnson retired to his bedroom. While talking with Lillie, Johnson had a stroke and fell to the floor. They got him into bed, but he regained consciousness and told them not to call a doctor. The next day another stroke killed him.

His funeral took place on August 3, 1875. Johnson had said many times that in death, he wanted his body wrapped in the flag with his head pillowed on the Constitution. These requests were followed. The body lay in state at his home on Main Street, then was taken to the courthouse to lie in state. The town was draped in black when the coffin was mounted on a wagon in front of the courthouse.

Johnson's funeral bier

Greene County Courthouse during Johnson's funeral

When Johnson died, the question arose, where was he to be buried? His death had been sudden: no funeral had been expected. Finally Sam gave them the answer—Signal Hill, where Johnson had often walked with Will or Sam. The funeral procession left the courthouse, passed the Johnson homeplace and was spread out from the gravesite to town when the casket reached the summit of Signal Hill.

At the gravesite, the Knights Templar formed the triangle and circle around the grave. The photograph of the burial shows the arriving mourners, with one side of the triangular formation of the Templars seen on the hilltop.

Johnson had devoted the last years of his life to the reconciliation of the sections and of the races, and the officials in charge of the funeral were chosen as if to symbolize reconciliation. The Parade Marshal was Henry H. Ingersoll, an attorney who came South after the war. Ingersoll's three assistants were: Confederate Col. Elbert Clay Reeves, Johnson's Private Secretary; Federal Maj. Augustus Herman Pettibone, a prominent attorney who had moved to Greeneville from Wisconsin; and Maj. James G. Reaves, who had been Sheriff of Greene County throughout the war and the change of regimes.

Thus Ingersoll was assisted by a Confederate officer, a Union officer, and the Civil War era Sheriff of Greene County who had functioned under both armies.

The pallbearers included prominent Greeneville and Greene County citizens: Johnson's close friend Blackston McDannel; O. B. Headrick, a relative of the Mayor of Greeneville during the Civil War; Alexander Benjamin Wilson, a veteran of the 4th Tennessee Union Infantry; Major James H. Robinson, 81st Tennessee Confederate Mounted Infantry, who had been Provost Marshal of Greene County during the last months of Confederate rule. The Confederates among the pallbearers also included Samuel E. Snapp, who had remained a civilian during the war, but had supported the

Greene County Courthouse during Johnson's funeral

Johnson's funeral on Main Street

Confederacy. Most were Unionists, but at least three ex-Confederates were among the officials and pallbearers. The pallbearers' names are traditional Greene County names: J. M. Sanders, O. B. Headrick. Wm. Davis, A. B. Wilson, C. L. Sevier, John M. McKee, C. H. Marsh, J. C. Hankins, L. W. Tipton, J. H. Robinson, Geo. E. Jones, Thos. J. Lane., James A. Galbraith, D. R. Britton, B. McDannel, E. Wilhoit, Samuel E. Snapp, L. W. McInturff.

Andrew Johnson had lived through troubled times, but he had the wit and energy to become a leader in his town, region, state and nation. When fate thrust him into the office of President, he stuck to his moral and legal principles and would not be moved by bribes or threats. Friend and foe agreed that Johnson was both honest and stubborn. His goal remained to ameliorate the living conditions of the great mass of the people and to bring them into the political system. President Johnson pardoned thousands of ex-rebels—the rank and file and lower leadership—to advance the cause of reconciliation.

While President, Johnson wanted to bring the races and sections of the country together in peace. He was not completely successful: presidents rarely are. But he did succeed in important ways. The nation survived, stayed united and eventually prospered; the nation was launched on its slow, fitful progress toward equal rights. And the Johnson Presidency contributed to this progress. During his presidency, the Thirteenth Amendment had been ratified, ending slavery in the United States of America; Johnson had consistently demanded that the ex-slaves' personal and property rights be protected, and the first Presidential election was held in which hundreds of thousands of black Americans voted. During his presidency, the United States remained at peace with the other nations of the world.

In many ways Johnson had fulfilled the promise of one of his finest declarations, spoken spontaneously in October 1864, in a speech freeing the slaves of Tennessee: "I speak now as one who feels the world is his country, and all who love equal rights his friends."

Senator Andrew Johnson and Family Caricature Silhouettes, 1843

Andrew Johnson Patterson, son of Martha Johnson Patterson and grandson of Andrew Johnson. Andrew Patterson was the father of Margaret Patterson Bartlett.

Andrew Johnson Jr., called "Frank"

**Andrew Johnson's office
on Summer Street, near Main Street.**

Martha Johnson Patterson

Andrew Johnson Monument
Greeneville, Tennessee

Sources for Chapter One
The Young Andrew Johnson

Several authors connected with Greeneville have written biographies of Andrew Johnson. The last eight chapters of Oliver Temple, *Notable Men of Tennessee*, 1899, constitute a Johnson biography by a Greene County native who knew Johnson well, often as a political opponent. James S. Jones, *Life of Andrew Johnson*, Greeneville, 1901, is the work of a Greeneville minister who knew many of the Johnson-Patterson family and some of his ex-slaves. Fay Warrington Brabson interviewed Greeneville citizens who had known Johnson; Brabson also examined papers held by the family for his *Andrew Johnson: a Life in Pursuit of the Right Course: 1808-1876*, Durham, N. C., 1972. Richard H. Doughty, *Greeneville: One Hundred Year Protrait, 1775-1875*, Greeneville, 1975, gives a word portrait of Greeneville in the Johnson years, preserving many local traditions of Johnson's life in Greeneville.

A number of Johnson biographies exist: John Savage, *The Life and Public Services of Andrew Johnson*, New York, 1866, interviewed Johnson while he was president and gave word portraits of him at work. Robert Winston, who published *Andrew Johnson: Plebian and Patriot*, New York, 1928, heard Johnson speak in Raleigh after he had retired from the Presidency. For his planned biography, Winston toured Greene County and interviewed many who had known Johnson. Winston's description of the youthful Eliza McCardle is quoted in the text.

Newspaperman George Fort Milton gave his masterful biography the strange title, *The Age of Hate*. Published in 1930, it is one of the best and most complete of Johnson biographies. Attorney Lloyd Paul Stryker, *Andrew Johnson: A Study in Courage*, New York, 1936, made a strong legal case for Johnson's innocence of the charges in the impeachment trial.

These early biographers present a generally positive view of Johnson, but some recent historians have been accusatory. Both Hans Trefousse, *Andrew Johnson: A Biography*, New York, 1989, and

David Warren Bowen, *Andrew Johnson and the Negro*, Knoxville, 1989, argue that Johnson was a racist out to subvert the civil rights of blacks, a view the present work seeks to refute.

Among modern scholars, objective studies of Johnson are found in the books of James Sefton, *Andrew Johnson and the Uses of Constitutional Power*, Boston, 1980, and *The United States Army and Reconstruction 1865-1877*, Baton Rouge, 1967. *The Papers of Andrew Johnson*, Knoxville, brings together 16 volumes of printed primary sources with annotations and commentary. This work is cited: *JP*, 7: 34, for volume 7, page 34.

The look of Greeneville College in the 1820s is described from the "Journal of Dr. Charles Coffin, 1820-1822," McClung Collection, Knox County Library, Knoxville, Tennessee; *Goodspeed's East Tennessee*, Nashville, 1887, 886ff; John E. Alexander, *Brief History of the Synod of Tennessee From 1817 to 1887*, Philadelphia, 1890. The intellectual outlook of the school can be found in the *Knoxville Gazette*, August 1, 1796; George M. Apperson, "The Emancipation and Ordination of a Tennessee Slave," *Presbyterian Voice*, September, 1999, and Sam Milligan, "Family Missal," MS, Tennessee State Archives, 17-20.

Good summaries of East Tennessee emancipation societies are found in Durwood Dunn, *An Abolitionist in the Appalachian South: Ezekiel Birdseye on Slavery, Capitalism, and Separate Statehood in East Tennessee, 1841-1842*, Knoxville, 1997, and Lester C. Lamons, *Blacks in Tennessee 1791-1970*, Knoxville, 1981.

Johnson's opposition to the anti-abolition law of 1836 is recorded in *Tennessee House of Representatives Journal*, 21st Assembly, 1st Session, 358, 462-3, 564-5. The petition Johnson presented in 1839 asking that certain slaves be freed and allowed to remain in Tennessee is: "Petition of Washington Henshaw and his wife Jane, and Samuel W. Doak, asking permission to emancipate certain slaves; referred to committee on judiciary," 1839.

Johnson speaking at the Greene County Courthouse is described in Temple, *Notable Men*, 373.

Will Johnson was interviewed in 1937 by Ernie Pyle, "A Former Slave Remembers," David Nichols, ed., *Ernie's America: the Best of Ernie Pyle's 1930s Travel Dispatches*, New York, 1989.

Nashville Whig, Thursday, January 20, 1842, p. 3, contains a summary of a Johnson speech on East Tennessee statehood.

Sources for Chapter Two
Abolitionist in Disguise

Johnson was called an "abolitionist in disguise" in Brownlow's *Whig*, October 26, 1842. Johnson's response is in *JP*, 1: 254.

Arthur Zilversmidt, *The First Emancipation: the Abolition of Slavery in the North*, U. of Chicago Press, 1967, examines gradual emancipation in the Northern states.

Johnson's attempt to redraw the congressional districts is in *JP*, 1: 85. His most extreme racial rhetoric is found in a congressional speech, *JP*, 1: 136, 140. The integrated meetings of the Democratic party are described by Brownlow, *The Jonesborough Whig*, December 4, 1844, p. 3; December 25, 1844, p. 5; January 1, 1845, p. 3.

Johnson's speeches quoted in this chapter include his Texas annexation speech, *JP*, 1: 205; his speech on the Homestead Bill, *JP*, 1: 300f; the First Inaugural speech, *JP*, 2: 172-183. Johnson's 1861 letter to Sam Milligan is printed in *JP*, 3: 160-61.

For an overview of events, Charles F. Bryan, "The Civil War in East Tennessee: A Social, Political and Economic History," Doctoral Dissertation, University of Tennessee, 1978.

Abolitionist Birdseye's 1861 letter to Johnson is published in Dunn, *Birdseye*, 270-71.

Sources for Chapter Three
The Civil War

Johnson's anti-secession tour of East Tennessee in 1861 is discussed in James Welch Patton, *Unionism and Reconstruction in Tennessee 1860-1869*, Chapel Hill, 1934, 53, and Winston, *Johnson*, 194-96. A local manuscript A. E. Newton Dobson, "Biography of Dr. and Mrs. A. S. N. Dobson of Limestone. R.F.D. of Broylesville, Tennessee," gives the Tusculum College story. Johnson's departure from Greeneville is from Winston, *Johnson*, 199, and Holtsinger to Johnson, *JP*, 12: 236-7.

The bridge burner campaign is discussed in Oliver Temple, *East Tennessee and the Civil War*, 375-79; Samuel W. Scott and Samuel P. Angel, *The History of the Thirteenth Tennessee Cavalry, U.S.A.*, Philadelphia, 1903; Donahue Bible, "Broken Vessels: The Story of the hanging of the 'Pottertown Bridge-Burners November-December 1861," MS, 1997; *War of the Rebellion: Official Records of the Union and Confederate Armies*, 128 vols., Series I, Volume 4: *passim*, hereafter cited: *OR*, I, 4: *passim*.

T. Harry Williams, "Andrew Johnson as a Member of the Committee on the Conduct of the War," *East Tennessee Historical Society Publications*, No. 12, 1940.

William Hesseltine, *Lincoln's Plan of Reconstruction*, Chicago, 1967, 60, notes that slaves freed after working on the Nashville fortifications included slaves of Unionists.

Johnson's connection to the assistance the East Tennessee and Virginia Railroad gave Burnside's invasion is discussed in the deposition of Wilson Willis, "Additional Matter in the case of Petition of the East Tennessee, Virginia and Georgia R.R. Co.," 385, Pam 859, Box 25, McClung Collection, Knox County Library. "Affairs of Southern Railroads," 39th Congress 2nd session, serial 1306, report 34 describes the operation in general.

Lerone Bennett Jr., *Forced into Glory: Abraham Lincoln's White Dream*, Chicago, 2000, is a well researched, but overly critical, study of Lincoln's conservative racial outlook. Bennett gives the entire text of the Emancipation Proclamation and points out its shortcomings.

Lincoln urged Johnson to recruit black regiments, March 26, 1863, *JP*, 6: 194-95. Johnson discussed the potential of blacks in freedom on several occasions, for example, *JP*, 6: 550, 582. General Lorenzo Thomas' efforts at black recruiting are summarized in Bell Irvin Wiley, *Southern Negroes, 1861-1865*, New Haven, 1965, 313, and in General Thomas' report, *OR*, III, 5: 119-24.

The "Eighth of August" emancipation day ceremonies are discussed in Robert Booker, *Two Hundred Years of Black Culture in Knoxville, Tennessee, 1791-1991*, the Donning Co., 1993, 88; Will Johnson describes the act of emancipation, "A Former Slave Remembers," *Ernie's America*.

The author interviewed Col. William D. Guinn of Greeneville on June 18, 2001, and Col. Guinn said that his father William McDonald Guinn told him that the date celebrated as Emancipation Day, the "Eight of August," was the day Johnson freed his personal slaves.

Johnson's Knoxville speech is in *JP*, 6: 671; his speech emancipating the Tennessee slaves, *JP*, 7: 251-53; the Vice Presidential Inaugural speech, *JP*, 7: 502-07.

Governor's Guard and the campaign in East Tennessee are discussed in *Thirteenth Tennessee*; *JP*, 7: 87.

Johnson and the constitutional convention of 1865 is described in Temple, *Notable Men*, 409-12.

Captain W. E. McElwee left a manuscript memoir of his conversation with Johnson just before his death. I have used the rough typescript in the McClung Collection, Knox County Library.

Sources for Chapter Four
President Johnson

Captain McElwee, typescript, McClung Collection, describes Johnson's emotion on hearing of Lincoln's assassination. Johnson's speech on being sworn as President, *JP*, 7: 553-54.

George Julian, *Political Recollections 1840 to 1872*, Chicago, 1884, 257, was present and published Ben Wade's "no trouble now" comment.

Philip S. Foner, *The Life and Writings of Frederick Douglass*, 4 vols., New York, 1955; Benjamin Quarles, *Frederick Douglass*, Washington, 1948, are two excellent Douglass biographies.

William Hanchett, *The Lincoln Murder Conspiracies*, Chicago, 1986, examines the Lincoln assassination.

The Lincoln-Johnson plan of reconstruction is discussed in Gideon Welles, *The Diary of Gideon* Welles, 3 vols., Boston, 1911, II, 290ff.

Johnson's letters concerning the 1865 elections are in *JP*, 5: 631; 11: 434.

On "black codes" John Hope Franklin, *Reconstruction: After the Civil War*, Chicago, 1961.

Johnson's integration of White House New Year's celebration is described in Welles, *Diary*, II, 410.

The Johnson-Douglass confrontation of 1866 is given in full in *JP*, 10: 41-48; for Johnson's angry remarks, Trefousse, *Johnson*, 242.

Johnson's veto messages, *JP*, 10: 125, 313-20.

Sefton, *Reconstruction*, 36, 43, discusses Johnson's approach to reconstruction law, including the Georgia hanging.

The conspiracies against Johnson are described in Milton, *Age of Hate*, 412, 414; *JP*, 12: 67f.

The Swing Around the Circle is summarized in Stryker, *Johnson*, 354-55; Milton, *Age of Hate*, Chapter XIV.

The legal conflict over ownership of the East Tennessee and Virginia Railroad are in "Affairs of Southern Railroads," 39th Congress, 2nd session; serial 1306, report 34.

Johnson's saving of the Nashville Methodist Church property is discussed in the brief memoir of E. C. Reeve, "The Real Andrew Johnson," Appendix, Stryker, *Johnson*.

Reconstruction legal cases can be examined in Greene County Courthouse records, microfilm, Cox Collection.

Bryan, "East Tennessee," describes the devastation left by the war.

Welles, *Diary*, *passim*, on discussions within the Johnson cabinet.

Sources for Chapter Five
Political Wars

Johnson's veto messages are found in *JP*, 10: 125, 313-320. Johnson's offer to Frederick Douglass is discussed in Foner, *Douglass*, IV, 204-05; Quarles, *Douglass*, 238.

Eric McKitrick, *Andrew Johnson and Reconstruction*, Chicago, 1960, 497.

Johnson's attitude toward race policy in summer 1867 is given in *JP*, 12: 506.

"Testimony taken before the Judiciary Committee of the House of Representatives in the Investigation of the Charges against Andrew Johnson," 39 Congress, 2nd session, 40th Congress, 1st session, 190-91, 1153.

The Third Annual Message is in *JP*, 13: 285-86; interview of December 1867, *JP*, 13: 396.

Welles, *Diary*, III, 279.

Trial of Andrew Johnson, 3 vols, Washington, 1868; Stryker, *Johnson*, gives a good analysis of the trial.

For Groesbeck's speech, *Trial*, I, 216-17.

On Johnson and New Orleans, *JP*, 15: 27-28, 86-88.

The number of whites disfranchised is discussed in Franklin, *Reconstruction*, 80, and Harold Faulkner, *American Political and Social History*, New York, 1952, 403.

Sources for Chapter Six
Ex-President and Senator Johnson

Johnson's return to Greeneville is described in Doughty, *Greeneville*, 249.

Robert Johnson's death is described in Ellen Robinson to "My dear Husband," May 25, 1869, James H. Robinson Papers, MS, Cox Collection, Greeneville-Greene County Library.

For Johnson's efforts to find his pre-war papers, *JP*, 16: 36, 37, 45, 73, and in James H. Robinson to Andrew Johnson, July 30, 1869, Andrew Johnson Papers, Library of Congress, a letter not included in *JP*, volume 16.

Johnson's meeting with E. C. Reeves is described in his "Johnson," Stryker, *Johnson*, 836.

JP, 16: 430f, gives Johnson's note of 1873.

Will Johnson, "An Ex-Slave Remembers," *Ernie's America*; Sam. Johnson to Andrew Johnson, *JP*, 12: 183.

Johnson's last speech, *JP*, 16: 713-46.

McElwee, Typescript, McClung Collection.

Johnson's death and funeral, Doughty *Greeneville*, 254-65; *JP*, 16: Appendix II.

Ad interim: temporary

Ameliorate: improve

Anglo-American: that which draws on British (Anglo) and American traditions

Baleful: evil, disastrous

De facto: existing in fact

Demos: the people

Demagogue: one who panders to a crowd

Disburse: pass out money

Disfranchise: to remove rights, especially voting rights

Emancipationist: one who favors freeing slaves

Enfranchise: giving the right to vote to someone

Obloquy: blame

Opiate: a medicine based on opium

President-elect: one who has been elected president but has not yet taken the office

Recusant: a non-conformist, one who refuses to follow authority

Suffrage: to be allowed to vote

Tariff: a tax on imported or exported goods, usually imported